# Making the Manifesto

# Making the Manifesto

## The Birth of
## Religious Humanism

William F. Schulz

**Skinner House Books**
Boston

Printed in Canada.

Cover design by Suzanne Morgan
Text design by Denise Hoffman

**Library of Congress Cataloging-in-Publication Data**

Schulz, William F.
    Making the manifesto : the birth of religious humanism /
    William F. Schulz.
       p.   cm.
    Includes bibliographical references and index.
    ISBN 1-55896-429-0 (alk. paper)
    1. Humanism, Religious—History—20th century.
  2. Humanist manifesto.   I. Humanist manifesto.   II. Title.

BL2747.6 .S38 2002
211'.6-dc21                    2002025133

10 9 8 7 6 5 4 3 2 1
05 04 03 02

The text of the Humanist Manifesto is reprinted with the permission
of the American Humanist Association.

*To R. Lanier Clance,
who has always followed his
own path and encouraged me
to find and follow mine.*

# Contents

# Foreword

Thanks to efforts by the Religious Right in the early years of the Reagan administration to locate and label some enemies of the republic "secular humanists," a revision of the Humanist Manifesto made headlines for a time in the 1980s. As had been true of so many other previous movements that questioned traditional religion, the foes of this movement succeeded in giving it more publicity than its supporters had ever been able to summon.

I welcome this book by William Schulz because it enters into the record a document and a mini-movement of which some have made too much and others, too little—while he is treating it about right. Those who have made too much include the heresy hunters and bush beaters, who have tried to track down and flush out a set of conspirators on whom they could blame the United States' moral flaws: abortion, opposition to school prayer, destruction of the family, insufficient patriotism, and more. These critics have a vision of a United States that was founded as and is to remain evangelically Protestant. True, there have been many immigrant intruders on Evangelicaldom. And the U.S. Supreme Court has been hard on those who have tried to bring it back by privileging, if not formally establishing, a Judeo-Christian (read "Evangelical") kingdom. Hollywood and the media have subverted what was left of that realm.

This assault on what the Right holds dear could not have been a natural development. Formal developers had to be involved. The drafters of the Humanist Manifesto would do just fine.

Thanks to such efforts, the heirs and surviving signers of the first Manifesto, so well introduced here by William Schulz, drew more headlines in 1980 than the pioneers. Those original signers were quite disappointed by the lack of reception granted their work in the secular and religious media and publics alike. One may argue that freethinkers, atheists, agnostics, skeptics, and other outsiders in religious America prosper best when they are most useful to their enemies. In 1933, Americans had other preoccupations, such as trying to survive the Depression, to distract them from fighting infidels. But around 1980, they found such humanists useful.

I welcome Schulz's work because I have been tracking the questioners and humanists since my graduate school days half a century ago. My doctoral dissertation was *The Uses of Infidelity: Free Thought and American Life*. It concentrated on periods during which freethinkers carried some weight, among them, the years surrounding the Declaration of Independence and the time of social experiment during Americans' move across the frontier.

Infidels were useful during the battle for separation of church and state, when antiestablishmentarian Baptists and their kin linked with Thomas Jefferson and others in a pragmatic alliance. Infidels also proved useful among the ancestors of the 1980s Religious Right—people of long ago who argued that the nation would self-destruct if government, on both national and state levels, were to let go of a formal religious establishment and not favor a particular religion or, on legal grounds, religion at all. The infidel or humanist then was a specter, a haunting and threatening figure. And religious liberals found the more radical humanists useful because they could say to the orthodox, "Look, you think our experimenting is dangerous, anti-God. Just look at the godless, and you'll see that we are quite respectable." Echoes of the work of such tacticians show up on the following pages in the lives of the more orthodox Unitarians.

The humanists, as here described, were puzzles to many unbelievers, casual agnostics, who wondered why anyone had to organize a movement of people who simply agreed with what the mainstream academy and scientists already professed. Why *religious* humanism? Why a *manifesto* for trophies of battles already won? We're not *exactly* about doing that, said authors of the Manifesto, but it looked to many as if they were inventing one more church body or taking over the one or two (Unitarian and Universalist) that were already safely in the camp of the non-God people. These humanists were more than puzzling; they were offensive to the conventionally religious, who thought, in effect, "We don't need the company of those who in their formal organizing tendencies look like a church but lack the main elements in them: God and respectability." While the movement trailed off during 1933 and 1934, the significant thinkers who were part of the Manifesto lived on and gave focus to religious thought that questioned convention.

Those who study denominational or revolutionary movement history will see something immediately recognizable about the people in Schulz's account: infighting. Denominations, designed to protect and propagate their members' specific beliefs, tend to be hosts to internal fracases. So it was with the religious humanists. Factionalism, schism, and fights over definition and strategy characterized much of the movement, and together, their impact gives life to the present account.

As noted earlier, one can make too much of the Humanist Manifesto. But humanists, the religious, scholars, and chroniclers of American life may also have made too little of it. Phenomena do not have to be large or long lasting to merit analysis. The signers of the Manifesto and those who fought for its acceptance provided landmarks that have helped historians and social analysts find their way in an American past that is never wholly gone.

These are not easy days in which to reappraise nontheist or antitheist religion. After September 11, 2001, when the United States entered a period that will be marked by a permanent sense of insecurity, the impulse to promote a "God Bless America" orthodoxy tends to relegate the humanists to the sidelines or to see them as out of step and even un-American. At such a time, the voice of the heterodox and the heretic merits a rehearing. It may be that some of the articulate questions of imposed uniformity "under God" can draw fresh inspiration from scrappy humanists who have thought through what a fulfilling and meaningful life could be without conventional religion.

William Schulz introduces that company and describes their impulses. He is fair in his treatment of their limits and on the side of those who see value in questioning—as did the signers of the Humanist Manifesto.

—Martin Marty

# Introduction

Whether they realize it or not, all Americans interested in matters religious, no matter what theological labels they claim, have been influenced by religious humanism, the movement whose origins in the early part of the twentieth century are described in this book. For those of orthodox persuasion, religious humanism—much less its counterpart, secular humanism—represents the stark danger that comes with abandonment of biblical authority. For more liberal Christians, religious humanism reflects a boundary that helps them define their own theological limits. And to those of a progressive stripe, regardless of whether they claim the humanist label themselves or are even interested in religion, humanism is of value to the extent that it embodies philosophical pragmatism with the conviction that is so germane to our current struggles: namely, that religious certitude leads to division, intolerance, and ultimately violence.[1]

Unitarian Universalism, the faith community in which the vast majority of religious humanists are found today, has, in particular, been deeply affected by the religious humanist strain, diverse as the theological perspectives may be within the Unitarian Universalist family. Foremost, religious humanism made it possible for those with radically nontraditional views of religion to find in Unitarian Universalism a comfortable religious home. Religious humanism was unapologetically *religious*. This is in contrast to the more secular form of humanism, as manifested today in the Council for Secular Humanism, for example, which has no truck at all with religious language, ritual, institutions, and leadership. The Humanist Manifesto of 1933, the preparation of which forms the backbone of this story, was consciously designed to encapsulate a religious faith,[2] not just a philosophy of life, and for all its religious failings, it represented a heartfelt attempt to amalgamate intellectual integrity with religious expression.

But religious humanism is not just a matter of historical curiosity, at least as far as Unitarian Universalism is concerned. After all, 46 percent of Unitarian Universalists reported in 1998 that they regarded themselves as theologically humanist—more than twice the number who identified with the second most common perspective, nature-centered spirituality, and far more than the 13 percent who called themselves theists or the 9.5 percent who described themselves as Christians.[3] And even those Unitarian Universalists who do not identify with the religious humanist category would be foolish not to realize that they, too, should pay it tribute, for it provides a set of values that are due honor to this day.

The truth is that a lot of nonsense passes for religion in this twenty-first century, as it has in all the preceding centuries. Religious humanism is willing to call a charlatan a charlatan, and while reason is by no means the only vehicle of religious exploration, we abandon it altogether only at our peril. Where would we who cherish the natural world be without religious humanism's insistence that the world is a seamless garment and that we humans are a part of the weaving? When the Unitarian Universalist Principles and Purposes revere the "interdependent web of all existence of which we are a part," they hark back to that fundamental humanist point, the second point in the Manifesto, that human beings are "a part of nature" and have "emerged as the result of a continuous process." Or consider religious humanism's courageous faith that the future of the world is in human hands—not those of an angry God or inexorable fate. Humanism beckons us to believe that we *can* make a difference to history. This is the source of my own passion for social justice. In fact, human rights themselves, as articulated in the Universal Declaration of Human Rights, are grounded not in the callings of the divine or the imperatives of natural law but in the common experience of human empathy transmogrified into a set of guidelines designed to effect a civilized world.[4] Finally, what kind of people would Unitarian Universalists be without humanism's generous contention that the blessings of life are available to all, not just the Chosen or the Saved, and that they appear not in the miraculous or extraordinary but in the simple dress of the everyday?

Religious humanism—particularly that version of it described by the 1933 Humanist Manifesto—has its limits, as we will see. Indeed, what system of thought that is now almost seventy years old would not? Interestingly enough, religious humanism contained the source of its own surpassing within its faith stance. "Any religion that can hope to be a . . . dynamic force . . . must be shaped by the needs of [its] age," the Manifesto proclaimed. There can be no doubt that the kind of religion the Manifesto advocated is now outdated. (Even die-hard humanists found a need to issue Manifestos II and III!) But what has supplanted it is still not entirely clear. By elucidating the origins of religious humanism, this book seeks to add to that clarity.

I was raised a third-generation Unitarian in Pittsburgh, Pennsylvania, by two Unitarian parents—but Unitarian parents of the very old school, theologically. My mother and I prayed together every night before I went to sleep, and my father believed he would be reunited with his parents and other deceased family members in something resembling heaven after death.

At age eleven, inspired by the election of John F. Kennedy and the burgeoning civil rights movement, I became intrigued by politics and have remained so ever since. But in my junior year in high school, thanks to the influence of a brilliant, dramatic English teacher named Barclay Palmer (a former Olympic shot-put athlete for Great Britain and great-grandson of the founders of the Salvation Army), I discovered religious questions. The whys and the wherefores began to supplement, if not displace, my interest in the hows and the whats. Barclay introduced my classmates and me to debate about the nature of the human creature, of evil, of death, and of God. He taught us the *Epic of Gilgamesh*, *The Inferno*, and *The Heart of Darkness*. He quoted from satirist Jonathan Swift and ethologist Konrad Lorenz, as well as from Shakespeare, the Koran, and the Bible. He took on the tough questions that other teachers seemed to duck. Most of all, he appeared to live his life with a degree of intensity, pathos, and passion that I had never seen in anyone before. And he did all this while identifying himself as a religious person, albeit not a conventional one.

My association with Barclay made me realize that it was time to return to the Unitarian (now also Universalist) Church that I had abandoned when I dropped out of church school in third grade. It was time to see what this religion business was all about. For the next few years, I attended Sunday services every week, read about religion voraciously, and talked to as many clergy as I could corner. At the end of it all, I decided to become a Unitarian Universalist minister. There was just one problem with my newly chosen profession: I didn't believe in God. In fact, I didn't believe in any of the religious things my parents did, such as prayer or heaven, and I really wasn't very interested in the Bible. I was interested in religious *questions* but not in the typical trappings of their *answers*. Could I possibly make it in the ministry? A host of humanist ministers—including the minister of my home church in Pittsburgh, Edward A. Cahill, and the minister I worked most closely with in college, R. Lanier Clance (later the founder of the First Existentialist Church of Atlanta and the person to whom this book is dedicated)—assured me that I could. The trick was to approach religion from the perspective of philosophy.

But a little philosophy, it has been said, is a dangerous thing. By the time I got to theological school, I was pretty well acquainted with the existential philosophers, and during my years at Meadville Lombard Theological School, the Unitarian Universalist seminary at the University of Chicago, I enrolled in as many philosophy courses and as few theology and Bible courses as I possibly could. I took particular interest in philosophy of religion, and at one time, I could recite, almost by heart, the refutations of each of Aquinas's five proofs for the existence of God. My newfound erudition convinced me that there was not even one respectable intellectual argument for traditional Christian belief. "Aha!" I can still hear myself cry. "But can God create a rock that is heavier than God can lift?" Only a resort to unsubstantial faith could rescue a theist from annihilation at the hands of a philosopher. I loved the story of a conversation between a philosopher and a theologian in which the theologian remarked that pursuing philosophy was as frustrating as a blind person looking in a dark room for a black cat that is not there, and the philosopher retorted, "Yes, and if I were a theologian, I'd find the cat." Such a retreat into irrationalism was not for the faint of heart. My classmates in theological school took to calling me "Bill, the Boy Humanist." In 1973, when I was twenty-three, I was rewarded for my nontheistic sanctity by being invited to become the youngest original signer of Humanist Manifesto II.

It is hardly surprising, then, that when it came time to choose the topic for my doctoral dissertation, the movement that had spawned the 1933 Humanist Manifesto—its history, sociology, and philosophical underpinnings—held rapt appeal. Furthermore, six of the thirty-four signers were still alive in 1974; I could therefore create a living history, a work of some original research. I would set out in quest of elderly humanists! The six all received me graciously and told me their stories.

But over the course of my four years at theological school, two other developments in my life worked their ways with me. One was that I entered psychotherapy, and the other was that my family started dying. The result of the former was that I came to have a far deeper appreciation for the irrational in every form and a far greater access to my own feelings, limitations, and yearnings than I had had before. Much of the Manifesto's humanism seemed pinched, even arrogant, and certainly too quickly dismissive of the vast realms of human experience that could not be reached by cognition alone. In a paradoxical kind of way, this type of *rationalism* seemed suitable only for the meek —that is, for those afraid to make the journey into the interior haunts of the unconscious, of guilt, passion, and pain. I knew from my experience with psychotherapy that the only way to get through emotional despair was to dive right into the midst of it, frightening as that might be. But humanism seemed to think (yes, that was the right word) that there might be a way around it.

For me, that confrontation with despair became most poignant in the quick succession of deaths of three of the five adults who had formed me as a human being, including my mother. An only child with but two remaining close blood relatives, I found the world a far more bleak and lonely place than the brave words of the Manifesto would allow: "Man will learn to face the crises of life in terms of his knowledge of their naturalness and probability. Reasonable and manly attitudes will be fostered by education and supported by custom." While I retained great respect for early religious humanism after I had finished the dissertation and graduated from theological school, as indeed I do today, these two experiences crystallized for me its limitations.

Over the years, I have seen those limitations ever more clearly, as the Manifesto implicitly predicted that I would. While the 1933 document had encouraged the "creative in man" and had proclaimed "nothing human [to be] alien to the religious," it had also ardently insisted that "the way to determine the existence and value of any and all realities is by means of intelligent inquiry" and that "religion must formulate its hopes and plans in the light of the scientific spirit and method." One of the signers, Oliver Reiser, had captured the essence of this perspective perfectly in a parody of a prayer:

> Thou Cosmic Movement, Cosmic Continuum! We petition thee to lend auditory discrimination to these, our laryngeal contractions. . . . May our cortical pathways always keep vigilance over our lower reflexes. May our endocrines not hypertrophy nor our hormones become toxic. . . . Increase our opsonic index. And though we walk through the valley of depressed metabolism, may we secrete no useless adrenaline.

Hard-edged, objective science could answer almost any question put to it. Werner Heisenberg had discovered his uncertainty principle in 1927, six years before the Manifesto was written, but quantum theory, with its profound implications for the limits of objectivity, had not yet gained the renown or acceptance it was to claim in later years. Yet even without the uncertainty principle, challenges to the Manifesto's presuppositions were easy to see.

If nothing human was truly alien to the religious, for example, then what are we to make of all the human experiences whose meanings could not be completely captured in scientific terms—dreams, for example, emotions, religious aspiration, wanton cruelty? And what are we to think of the animal world? Are even the greatest apes nothing more than automatons? Of course, all this could be reduced to physiological phenomena, as Roy Wood Sellars, the Manifesto's original author, suggested they should be, but anyone who tried to capture the holistic significance of love or loyalty, guilt or grandeur, in terms of brain cell functioning alone could be rightly accused of displaying a pitiful paucity of imagination. A brain-imaging machine called SPECT has recently been used to identify changes in the top-rear part of the cerebellum brought about by meditation. When it is deprived of sensory input, the so-called orientation area—the part of the brain that monitors where the self ends and the rest of the world begins—quiets down, and the individual is left with a feeling of being one with God or with the Cosmos.[5] A traditional humanist might cite such research as evidence that the experience of God is illusory, but the evidence could just as easily be read to support the notion that the *phenomenon* of feeling one with the Whole is a profound reality with arguably beneficial side effects, the full meaning of which cannot be captured by intelligent inquiry alone. Surely, this is what poet Wallace Stevens was pointing to when he said that "the truth depends upon a walk around a lake."

Science is by no means an enemy of imagination. As Alfred North Whitehead pointed out as early as 1929, science begins in wonder and is advanced through the audacity of intuition.[6] But the humanists tended to be the practical sort, whose first question of any new scientific development was: And what can this do for us humans? This left them extraordinarily vulnerable when the answer came back: It can kill you. With the coming of the Second World War only a few short years after the Manifesto was published, the world would be reminded—in the form of the Nazi's V2 rockets and efficient gas chambers, to say nothing of the Allies' atomic bomb—that science and technology could foster massive amounts of destruction as readily as they could relieve human suffering. A few of the religious humanists had anticipated technology's terrifying possibilities, but the general tenor of the movement, convinced as it was that salvation lay largely in molding nature to human needs, was unrestrained in its enthusiasm for technological manipulations and unprepared for the devastating consequences such manipulation could unleash.

That was, in part, because early religious humanism lacked a clear doctrine of human freedom—not political freedom, which it wholeheartedly endorsed, but free agency, what was traditionally called *free will*. Hence, it lacked an adequate understanding of evil. Indeed, it is curious that the Manifesto makes not a single mention of the human capacity for free choice. On the contrary, it seems to suggest a brand of cultural determinism in its affirmation that "man's religious culture and civilization . . . are the product of a gradual development due to his interaction with his natural environment and with his social heritage. The individual born into a particular culture is largely molded to that culture." If that is all there is to it, then the religion embodied in the Manifesto is little better than a product of cultural dictation.[7] But quite apart from this confoundment, without a belief in some measure of free choice, the Manifesto was hard pressed to fully account for human evil. Not surprisingly, it had little to offer in the way of consolation from anguish. It tended to forget that religion was not just about insight but also about poetry, that culture was reflected not only in its world view but also in its music.

In all my conversations with the signers of the Manifesto, none of them, except Lester Mondale, ever talked about religion in terms of *experience;* they talked exclusively in terms of *beliefs.* But religion is also about longing and lament, laughter and light. As George Santayana put it, "Religion is the love of life in the consciousness of its impotence." Moreover, it requires a resource suitable to the plight of Winnie the Pooh who, when stuck in the doorway of Rabbit's house, made a simple request: "Would you be so kind as to read a Sustaining Book such as would help and comfort a Wedged Bear in a Great Tightness?" In large measure, humanism lacked such a "book." It could explain Pooh's plight—maybe even tell him how to extract himself from it.   But humanism fell mute on those occasions when Pooh was good and truly *stuck*, in the face of evil and heartache and death, when the only response worthy of the occasion was to curse the human plight and be determined to dance nonetheless. While humanism gave a nod to art, it lacked an aesthetic sense; its language was crisp, but its rhythm was flat. It had little, if anything, to offer to those who brooked consternation before chaos or treasured awe before vastness. Some of the early religious humanists, including Lester Mondale and John Herman Randall Jr., recognized this, but they belonged to a distinct minority.

Henry Ward Beecher once concluded a sermon with a magnificent peroration describing the Angel of Truth holding a spear tipped with a star. Afterward an admiring parishioner exclaimed, "Oh, Dr. Beecher, how did you happen to think of the star, the spear tipped with the star?" Beecher replied, "I didn't think of it; *I saw it!*" Most of the early religious humanists, finding metaphor dangerous, would have had no idea what Beecher was talking about.

Critical as I became of the traditional humanist stance, a brand of religious humanism has, nonetheless, accompanied me throughout my ministry, my service to the Unitarian Universalist Association, and, indeed, my years at Amnesty International—all of it presaged by the early religious humanism described in this book. That is one reason I accepted from the American Humanist Association (AHA) in 2000 the Humanist of the Year Award, previous recipients of which include far greater luminaries than I, such as Isaac Asimov and Stephen J. Gould. I felt a little guilty accepting the award on two counts: First, I am often uncomfortable with the kind of humanism, reflected in some quarters of the AHA, that holds religion in general in disdain. (On the other hand, I am closer to the humanist perspective than to that of the evangelical Pray 365 Project, which quite inaccurately named me one of the world's 365 most influential people just a few weeks before. I figured the AHA designation would help balance things out.)

The second reason for my guilt is that Unitarian Universalism, by becoming a home for religious humanists, has contributed to the difficulty humanism has experienced in its efforts to flourish as a stand-alone movement. It was, after all, the dream of many humanist pioneers to found a potent humanist institution independent of any other. But that dream has not been realized. The AHA today has but a few thousand members. Unitarian Universalism has over two-hundred thousand, 46 percent of whom, as we have seen, identify themselves as humanists. And I have contributed to that assimilation. As president of the Unitarian Universalist Association from 1985 to 1993, I tried to make humanists feel at home in the Association, which, despite their considerable numbers, they often do not. As Unitarian Universalism has discovered spirituality and made room for a variety of religious lexicons, those of traditional humanist persuasion have often become uncomfortable. Why is that?

Part of the answer is that many of the traditionalists are now elderly (the 1998 survey of Unitarian Universalists revealed that the older the respondent, the more likely he or she is to be a humanist) and fear that the number of humanists is dwindling. Other explanations include the traditionalists' negative experiences with other religious traditions and their understanding of the heritage they embody as one that rejects all things religious. But this last perception is simply wrong. Most of the early religious humanists were not interested in abandoning religion but in transforming it. Moreover, they did not want to impose their views on Unitarians. Their goal, as I have said, was to form a separate organization. What those who identified themselves as Unitarians asked of their denomination was not that it rid itself of other theological perspectives but that it make room for theirs. How ironic, then, that some of humanism's contemporary practitioners would be the most resistant to an evolving faith, and how paradoxical that some of those whose humanist forebears fought the battle for theological pluralism within the Unitarian fold are today the agents of a narrow sectarianism.

I have long thought that if all of us understood better where religious humanism came from—the battles it fought, the assumptions it purchased, the victories it claimed, and the limitations it fostered—we would be better equipped today to integrate its theology into our religious world view, to draw the best from its inspiration, and to avoid the pitfalls to which it once succumbed. Besides, the story of the birth of religious humanism is a fascinating one, ripe with drama and tinged with humor. It is philosophically challenging and sociologically revealing.

This book would never have come to fruition, made the leap from dissertation to text, without the encouragement of my wife, Rev. Beth Graham of Huntington, New York, or the editorial expertise of Mary

*humanism lacked the humanities*

Benard of the Unitarian Universalist Association staff. Even so, it bears
some of the handicaps of its origins.

Much of the *quoted* language is gender insensitive in a way that we
have long since eschewed. Furthermore, there are virtually no women
mentioned in the book. The explanation for both of these facts is that
there were no women prominently involved in the founding of the religious humanist movement nor did the pioneers seem to notice their
absence. (Even today, the leadership of the American Humanist Association, astonishingly, is largely male.) Nothing could be more ironically
illustrative of the Manifesto's own point that "the individual born into a
particular culture is largely molded to that culture," and I cannot help
but believe that early religious humanism suffered for its narrowness.
Would it have been as blind to the experiential dimension of life, to take
just one example, or as dismissive of others' points of view if women
had played a role in its formulation?

That no people of color sat at the table of early religious humanist
leadership almost goes without saying. Yet it must be said, given what
we know of "black pioneers in a white denomination," including the fact
that Lewis McGee, an African American, proclaimed himself a humanist
in 1927 and sought to enter the Unitarian ministry but was discouraged
by Curtis Reese, who told him, "You'll have to bring your own church."[8]
I have often asked myself whether I would have chosen this dissertation
topic had I been as conscious of sexism and racism in 1974 as I hope I
am today. Regardless of the answer, early religious humanism's lacunae
are glaring, even if it did address class issues in a way that was remarkable for its day.

I gratefully acknowledge those who helped make my dissertation
possible, including the seven signers I interviewed,[9] one of whom, the
late Edwin H. Wilson, opened his home and files to me for over a solid
week in 1973.[10] Those who advised me on the preparation of the dissertation during my days at Meadville Lombard—both informally (the late
James Luther Adams, who, by the way, held humanism in considerable
disdain) and formally (the late John Godbey and Ron Engel, still very
much with us)—also deserve a mention.

The humanist-theist controversy described in this book has long since
been over, not just within Unitarian Universalism but, indeed, the larger
world. In one sense, that is because Jerry Falwell and Pat Robertson are
right: The basic principles of humanism have come to pervade our larger

culture. In a recent pamphlet on humanism, one of its practitioners listed its basic tenets as these:

Showing love to all humans.

Immortality is found in the examples we set and the work we do.

We gain insight from many sources and all cultures. . . .

We have the power within ourselves to realize the best we are capable of as human beings.

We are responsible for what we do and become.[11]

Of course, nothing is wrong with any of these affirmations. I agree with all of them. But I would venture to say that so do millions of other Americans, who would be shocked to learn that they are thereby considered humanists. I doubt if there is a single theist, Christian, or advocate of earth-centered spirituality within Unitarian Universalism today who would *not* affirm these tenets. Most of them would just not stop there.

Informed by such latter-day influences as feminist theology, Zen Buddhism, deep ecology, and new models of cosmology introduced by science itself, most religious explorers today would want to go further, use richer language, and wrestle with deeper questions. And therein lies another reason the humanist-theist controversy is behind us: The religious world—and not just the Unitarian Universalist religious world—has largely said to such explorers, "Go to it."

That sanction includes a willingness to employ a wider lexicon of traditional religious language than that with which the early religious humanists would have been comfortable. Thomas Carlyle said, "Life is one long quarrel with God but we make up in the end." My life has followed that trajectory as well, although in a far different vein than Carlyle intended. It is not particularly important to me anymore whether I or anyone else uses "God talk." What is of supreme importance is that I live my life in a posture of gratitude—that I recognize my existence and, indeed, Being itself, as an unaccountable blessing, a gift of grace. Sometimes, it is helpful to call the source or fact of that grace *God* and sometimes not. But what is always helpful and absolutely necessary is to look kindly on the world, to be bold in pursuit of its repair, and to be comfortable in the embrace of its splendor. I know no better term for what I seek than an encounter with the Holy.

　　Someone has categorized religions along a spectrum from the monkey-hold type, on one end, to the cat-hold brand, on the other. In *monkey-hold religion*, the babies cling to Mama as she strides through the world; whether they live or die depends, in good measure, on their own dexterity. In *cat-hold religion*, Mama holds babies by the scruffs of their necks, dangling them over the abyss; their calling is largely to take on a healthy dose of trust and enjoy the scenery. Early religious humanism was monkey-hold religion, through and through. Today, we recognize more readily the wisdom of the feline faith.

　　But having said all this, I return, in the last measure, to appreciation. For of course, early religious humanists had to be bold in their pronouncements and brash in their claims. They were seeking nothing less than to save religion itself—from the modernists, on the one hand (whom they thought would turn it to mush), and the futilitarians, on the other (whom they knew would throw it out altogether). In that task, they succeeded by carving out a spot for an intellectually respectable faith. And for that, every one of us owes them our thanks.

# Text of the
# Humanist Manifesto
## 1933

THE TIME HAS COME for widespread recognition of the radical changes in religious beliefs throughout the modern world. The time is past for mere revision of traditional attitudes. Science and economic change have disrupted the old beliefs. Religions the world over are under the necessity of coming to terms with new conditions created by a vastly increased knowledge and experience. In every field of human activity, the vital movement is now in the direction of a candid and explicit humanism. In order that religious humanism may be better understood we, the undersigned, desire to make certain affirmations which we believe the facts of our contemporary life demonstrate.

THERE IS GREAT DANGER of a final, and we believe fatal, identification of the word *religion* with doctrines and methods which have lost their significance and which are powerless to solve the problem of human living in the Twentieth Century. Religions have always been means for realizing the highest values of life. Their end has been accomplished through the interpretation of the total environing situation (theology or world view), the sense of values resulting therefrom (goal or ideal), and the technique (cult), established for realizing the satisfactory life. A change in any of these factors results in alteration of the outward forms of religion. This fact explains the changefulness of religions through the centuries. But through all changes religion itself remains constant in its quest for abiding values, an inseparable feature of human life.

TODAY MAN'S LARGER UNDERSTANDING of the universe, his scientific achievements, and his deeper appreciation of brotherhood, have created a situation which requires a new statement of the means and purposes of religion. Such a vital, fearless, and frank religion capable of furnishing adequate social goals and personal satisfactions may appear to many people as a complete break with the past. While this age does owe a vast debt to the traditional religions, it is nonetheless obvious that any religion that can hope to be a synthesizing and dynamic force for today must be shaped for the needs of this age. To establish such a religion is a major necessity of the present. It is a responsibility which rests upon this generation. We therefore affirm the following:

FIRST:  Religious humanists regard the universe as self-existing and not created.

SECOND:  Humanism believes that man is a part of nature and that he has emerged as the result of a continuous process.

THIRD:  Holding an organic view of life, humanists find that the traditional dualism of mind and body must be rejected.

FOURTH:  Humanism recognizes that man's religious culture and civilization, as clearly depicted by anthropology and history, are the product of a gradual development due to his interaction with his natural environment and with his social heritage. The individual born into a particular culture is largely molded into that culture.

FIFTH:  Humanism asserts that the nature of the universe depicted by modern science makes unacceptable any supernatural or cosmic guarantees of human values. Obviously humanism does not deny the possibility of realities as yet undiscovered, but it does insist that the way to determine the existence and value of any and all realities is by means of intelligent inquiry and by the assessment of their relation to human needs. Religion must formulate its hopes and plans in the light of the scientific spirit and method.

SIXTH:  We are convinced that the time has passed for theism, deism, modernism, and the several varieties of "new thought."

SEVENTH:  Religion consists of those actions, purposes, and experiences which are humanly significant. Nothing human is alien to the religious. It includes labor, art, science, philosophy, love, friendship, recreation—all that is in its degree expressive of intelligently satisfying living. The distinction between the sacred and the secular can no longer be maintained.

EIGHTH:  Religious humanism considers the complete realization of human personality to be the end of man's life and seeks its development and fulfillment in the here and now. This is the explanation of the humanist's social passion.

NINTH:  In place of the old attitudes involved in worship and prayer the humanist finds his religious emotions expressed in a heightened sense of personal life and in a cooperative effort to promote social well-being.

TENTH:  It follows that there will be no uniquely religious emotions and attitudes of the kind hitherto associated with belief in the supernatural.

ELEVENTH:  Man will learn to face the crises of life in terms of his knowledge of their naturalness and probability. Reasonable and manly attitudes will be fostered by education and supported by custom. We assume that humanism will take the path of social and mental hygiene and discourage sentimental and unreal hopes and wishful thinking.

TWELFTH:  Believing that religion must work increasingly for joy in living, religious humanists aim to foster the creative in man and to encourage achievements that add to the satisfactions of life.

THIRTEENTH:  Religious humanism maintains that all associations and institutions exist for the fulfillment of human life. The intelligent evaluation, transformation, control, and direction of such associations and institutions with a view to the enhancement of human life is the purpose and program of humanism. Certainly religious institutions, their ritualistic forms, ecclesiastical methods, and communal activities must be reconstituted as rapidly as experience allows, in order to function effectively in the modern world.

FOURTEENTH:  The humanists are firmly convinced that existing acquisitive and profit-motivated society has shown itself to be inadequate and that a radical change in methods, controls, and motives must be instituted. A socialized and cooperative economic order must be established to the end that the equitable distribution of the means of life be possible. The goal of humanism is a free and universal society in which people voluntarily and intelligently cooperate for the common good. Humanists demand a shared life in a shared world.

FIFTEENTH AND LAST:  We assert that humanism will: (a) affirm life rather than deny it; (b) seek to elicit the possibilities of life, not flee from it; and (c) endeavor to establish the conditions of a satisfactory life for all, not merely for the few. By this positive *morale* and intention humanism will be guided, and from this perspective and alignment the techniques and efforts of humanism will flow.

SO STAND THE THESES OF religious humanism. Though we consider the religious forms and ideas of our fathers no longer adequate, the quest for the good life is still the central task for mankind. Man is at last becoming aware that he alone is responsible for the realization of the world of his dreams, that he has within himself the power for its achievement. He must set intelligence and will to the task.

*Signers:*

    Johannes Abraham Christoffel Fagginer Auer
    Edwin Burdette Backus
    Harry Elmer Barnes
    Leon Milton Birkhead
    Raymond Bennett Bragg
    Edwin Arthur Burtt
    Ernest Caldecott
    Anton J. Carlson
    John Dewey
    Albert C. Dieffenbach
    John Dietrich
    Bernard Fantus
    William Floyd
    Frank Hankins
    Eustace Haydon
    John Haynes Holmes
    Llewelyn Jones
    Robert Morse Lovett
    Harold Parsons Marley
    Lester Mondale
    Charles Francis Potter
    John Herman Randall Jr.
    Curtis Reese
    Oliver Reiser
    Clinton Lee Scott
    Roy Wood Sellars
    Harlow Shapley
    Maynard Shipley
    W. Frank Swift
    Vivian T. Thayer
    Eldred Cornelius Vanderlaan
    Joseph Walker
    Jacob J. Weinstein
    Frank Scott Corey Wicks
    David Rhys Williams
    Edwin Henry Wilson

# The Roots of
# Religious Humanism

God dies only for a few. Over time, God may well change form for many people, from personal to vague to immanent, from transcendent to omnipotent to limited. But in American culture, at least, God *dies* only for a few. "Whither is God," cried Friedrich Nietzsche's madman. "I shall tell you. We have killed him—you and I." But the people only stared in astonishment. "I come too early," said the madman. "This tremendous event . . . has not yet reached the ears of man." (And that was in 1882!) Even so, the madman's cry has reached *some* ears in every generation since. And for those, the madman had a question: "Must not we ourselves become gods simply to seem worthy of [God's death]?"[1] When God is gone, faith turns to humanity.

This is the story of those who, in the third and fourth decades of the twentieth century, heard Nietzsche's call and heeded Nietzsche's question. This is the story of *religious humanism:* a religious movement that emphasized human capabilities, especially the human capacity to reason; that adopted the scientific method to search for truth; and that promoted the right of all humans to develop to their full potential. It is the story of a movement that sought to construct what Rev. John Dietrich called a "religion without God," shifting the focus of religious faith from divinity to humanity. Clergy and journalists, philosophers and scientists banded together, refusing to believe that human beings could not be saved and insisting that they themselves would be the instrument of salvation.

Religious humanism has its roots deep in antiquity, in Francis Bacon and René Descartes, in deism and the teachings of the *philosophes.* But the focus of this tale is on the movement as it developed in the United States, a movement whose faith was best summarized in the

1

Humanist Manifesto of 1933. It is fitting, then, to begin by looking at
the intellectual, religious, and cultural world that was the United States
in the early 1900s.

## The Intellectual Context: Science and Evolution

The Western world of thought was in the midst of turmoil and flux as it
approached the end of the nineteenth century. Two developments had
shaped its intellectual ethos: (1) the emergence of science as a respected
discipline for the ascertainment of fact and alteration of the world and
(2) the acceptance of evolution as a valid explanation of growth and
change on a multitude of levels.

Since the eighteenth century, serious philosophers had been
roughly divided into two schools of thought when it came to the conflict between science and religion. The more scientifically minded
insisted that the objects of religious inquiry were beyond the range of
reason and that only positivism (that is, knowledge verified by the
empirical sciences) held any promise for the improvement of humankind. This view was the progenitor of twentieth-century naturalism and
of what came to be called religious humanism. The other school of
thought generally admitted that the existence of religious ultimates,
such as God, could not be proved but urged that those ultimates be
acknowledged for the benefits that would accrue from such beliefs—
benefits such as comfort in the face of human mortality. The flourishing
of the first view—the positivist view—is of most interest in this work,
for it provided an atmosphere conducive to the emergence of science as
a predominant mode of human thought.

To a large extent, the development of science as a vital world force
was a simple matter of fact. The nineteenth century was a time of out-
standing scientific advances. Louis Pasteur's discoveries revolutionized
hygiene, Matthias Schleiden and Theodor Schwann developed what is
now known as cell theory, and Marie and Pierre Curie discovered
radium. Even the laying of the transatlantic cable contributed to the
growing popular conviction that science worked. It provided explanations and improvements where none had existed before. By the turn of
the century, positivism had attained immense respectability—but such
respect did not come without controversy.

No scientific proposition occasioned more debate than Charles
Darwin's 1859 introduction of the theory of evolution and natural
selection. It is not an exaggeration to say that this conflict influenced the

whole tenor of the period. Among those who took evolution seriously, two camps emerged that were not dissimilar to those that characterized the science and religion divide. On the one hand, there were those who took evolution to be the process by which growth and change came about, and on the other, those who, while often accepting the first view, saw evolution as an empirically verifiable manifestation of God. In the twentieth century, religious humanism would arise out of the former perspective and Protestant modernism out of the latter.

Perhaps the paragon of the first view was the English biologist Thomas Henry Huxley, whose importance for religious humanism can hardly be overstated. An ardent advocate of evolution (nicknamed "Darwin's bulldog" for the ferocity with which he promoted the theory), Huxley was most of all a radically honest man who refused to entertain any belief of which science would not approve. Moreover, he found that most of the quandaries he confronted were ones that science could not yet answer. In light of that, he simply acknowledged that he lacked insight in many areas and would have to stand as an agnostic (a term he coined) on many issues of interest to the human mind. This was particularly true with regard to questions of religious knowledge, and Huxley quickly discovered that to honor his convictions, he would have to forego religious faith. In his essay "Agnosticism," Huxley explained that his stand was not a substitute for religion; not a creed, but a method,

> the essence of which lies in the rigorous application of a single principle . . . [that is,] "try all things, hold fast that which is good." It is the foundation of the Reformation which simply illustrated the axiom that every man should be able to give a reason for the faith that is in him; it is the great principle of Descartes; it is the fundamental principle of modern science. Positively the principle may be expressed: In matters of the intellect, follow reason as far as it will take you without regard to any other consideration. And negatively . . . do not pretend that conclusions are certain which are not demonstrated or demonstrable.[2]

Huxley represents the nineteenth-century apex of the empirical revolution that Bacon had begun so many centuries before. The agnostic was committed first of all to truth, and truth was only that which could be experimentally tested. All metaempirical beliefs, therefore, were beyond the bounds of intellectual integrity.

One of the most interesting aspects of Huxley's thought was his attitude toward morals. Concerned as he was to deny that ethical behavior depended upon belief in supernatural rewards and punishments, he was, at the same time, not convinced that evolution offered assurances of moral progress either. To the contrary, the ethical process is one that may even be at odds with the evolutionary for, in contradiction to natural selection, ethics encourages cooperation and seeks to minimize suffering. Huxley saw no trace of moral purpose in nature; morality was a human creation. And if morality was to overcome nature, it required the assistance of science and intelligence. The similarity between Huxley's view and the faith of twentieth-century religious humanism will soon become evident.

But there was another, largely theological response to Darwin's theory, one that viewed evolution as a working out of God's plan. American historian and philosopher John Fiske, among others, promoted the perspective that was to become Protestant modernism. In his 1899 essay "Through Nature to God," Fiske set out to reconcile evolution with divine power by boldly asserting that the evolutionary mechanism was the agency of that power. Evolution was evidence of God's glory as manifested by the fact that evolution implied the perfectibility of humankind. Fiske also believed that moral evil was a feature of a lower state of being—unfortunate, to be sure, but indispensable, as well, since evil was required if human beings were ever to know good. Altruism would gradually come to predominate in human culture as evolution carried human development to higher and higher moral levels, until human beings assumed the image of God. The difference in tone between Fiske's view and Huxley's is all too clear.

In sum, science and evolution ushered in both a sophisticated naturalism (which, in turn, provided the grounding for a rationalistic religious faith) and, at the same time, sharply altered liberal Christianity. But science and evolution were not the only phenomena that threatened religious orthodoxy.

## The Religious Context: Modernism and Free Thought

In addition to the issue of evolution, liberals felt called upon to respond to new ideas in biblical studies, psychology, and anthropology. The year 1835 saw the publication of German theologian David Friedrich Strauss's seminal work, *The Life of Jesus.* No longer content to regard biblical history as fundamentally different from secular, Strauss and other scholars sought to understand miracles in naturalistic and symbolic ways. Such higher criticism interpreted the Scriptures in the same way it did other historical documents, with no special dispensation from the requirements of consistency, accuracy, and supportive evidence. This scholarship discouraged literal interpretations and forced Christian apologists to reevaluate the issue of biblical authority.

The publication of German philosopher Ludwig Feuerbach's *The Essence of Christianity* in 1855 reflected a second challenge to conventional views of religion in that it attempted to understand divinity as a projection of human beings' most primitive needs, desires, and fears. "The divine essence," Feuerbach wrote, "is nothing else than the human essence . . . isolated from the limitations of the individual. . . . Thus all the attributes of the divine essence are attributes of the essence of man."[3]

Although Feuerbach's work was hardly noticed by American Protestantism, its significance is that it foreshadowed the more devastating critique of religion offered by an Austrian some half-century later. Sigmund Freud not only challenged the Christian assumption of psychological independence and human free agency, but in his little classic *The Future of an Illusion*, he argued that God was little more than a projection of human fears and wishes. The psychoanalytic revolution, debatable though its first principles may have been, was something no educated person could ignore.

A third major blow to Christianity occurred with the appearance of Scottish anthropologist James Frazer's masterpiece, *The Golden Bough*. Originally published in Scotland in 1890, an abridged, one-volume edition was released in the United States in 1923. Frazer's massive study of folklore, magic, and religion showed the similarities between the beliefs and rituals of early cultures and those of Christianity. Was Christianity little more than an adaptive form of animism?

These three developments, then—in addition to the impact of science and evolution—shaped the religious mood of the United States at the turn of the century and drove most religious intellectuals into some form of either skepticism, popularly dubbed *free thought*, or Christian liberalism, known at the time as *modernism*.

Protestant modernism represented those relatively sophisticated people who were prepared to defend the Christian faith but were also concerned with maintaining their academic credibility. They rejected an anthropomorphic concept of God in favor of an immanent one, the authority of the Bible in favor of human reason and experience, and otherworldly concerns in favor of this world as the center of action.

Science had eliminated the traditional discontinuity between the super-natural and the worldly; modernism sought to reconstruct a doctrine of God consistent with the natural. God was to be the source of life, the Whole, identical with, not superordinate to, the cosmic process. There was no room for supernaturalism, no place for miracles.

In *The Meaning of Faith*, published in 1919, Harry Emerson Fosdick—professor of practical theology at Union Theological Seminary, minister of Riverside Church in New York City, and a popular spokes-person for modernism—wrote, "[The Christian] takes the full orb of personality, self-conscious being that knows and purposes and loves, and he affirms that God is most like this."[4] For Fosdick, God is *like* personal-ity but not equivalent to it, an ultimate power beyond humanity. The New York minister was not a systematic theologian, however, and failed to specify just how or what God is.

Walter Lippmann identified the problem quickly in his *A Preface to Morals*, published in 1929: "Search the writings of liberal churchmen, and when you come to the crucial passages which are intended to express their belief in God, you will find . . . that at just this point their uncertainty is most evident."[5] This tension and confusion was one of the factors that led to the undoing of modernism.

And if God was hard to define, what was the modernists' source of religious authority? According to contemporary scholar Kenneth Cauthen, "Liberal theology rejected any arbitrary appeal to external authority [revelation] and insisted that all religious affirmations must be grounded in, or at least subject to confirmation by, the data of religious experience or the conclusions of reason."[6] No longer would biblical or ecclesiastical injunctions do; religious principles that violated the intel-lectual canons of reasonable persons were suspect. For modernism, reli-gious authority was said to be derived largely, if not solely, from experience within the natural order.

This, in turn, led quite easily to an emphasis on improving the world. Near the close of the nineteenth century, there arose among lib-eral Christians a newfound commitment to political and social justice known as the *social gospel*, a commitment directly traceable to the influ-ence of science and evolution. Practical, not speculative, theology became the liberal norm. Evolution and the accompanying notion of inevitable moral progress led to the assumption that societies as well as individuals could be redeemed. And sin was accounted for largely on the basis of external and impersonal mechanisms of nature that cramped innate human goodness and perverted it unnecessarily into evil.

Sin, said Fosdick, represents the struggle between the higher and the lower parts of the self. Humans are basically good, but they are held back by natural tendencies. Even so, as long as they can set ideals, feel remorse, and struggle to make life better, there is something divine about humans, something of infinite worth.

Henry Steele Commager has analyzed the decline of modernism (which he labeled "liberalism") cogently: "Religion came to be largely a matter of observing certain formalities and doing good. . . . The difficulty with such liberalism . . . was that it tended to become increasingly secular. . . . [L]iberals in religion found it more convenient to practice their ethics . . . without benefit of church affiliation."[7]

Religious humanism took a position immediately to the left of liberal Christianity. It retained its religious proclivities but was not entirely divorced from the free-thought tradition; indeed, it took up some of the slack in the twentieth century where blatant agnosticism had left off in the nineteenth. In its early stages, nineteenth-century agnosticism, or free thought, captured the loyalty of a surprising number of people. Indeed, it is fair to say that an undercurrent of skepticism, explicitly nontheistic or otherwise, has played across the American intellectual scene throughout the nation's history.

The most consistent, hard-nosed, and notorious nineteenth-century American skeptic was the indefatigable orator and lawyer Colonel Robert Green ("Royal Bob") Ingersoll. A patrician on political matters, an economic reactionary, counselor to Republican pols and presidents, Ingersoll echoed the familiar orthodoxies of his day on most issues except the theological, upon which he could hardly be equalled at sophisticated blasphemy. Between 1869 and his death in 1899, Ingersoll pronounced his Huxleyan skepticism to large and enthusiastic crowds in virtually every major city in the land. Preaching principles of reason, observation, and experience, Ingersoll became the focal point of heretical controversy, with his lectures and criticisms answered by clergy across the nation. Try as they might, however, to diminish the Colonel's popularity, Ingersoll's charm, wit, and ingenuity (as well, no doubt, as his utterly respectable positions on so many nontheological questions) held him in good stead for more than a generation.

Yet American society hardly witnessed mass conversions to unbelief. This discrepancy between the popular regard shown to Ingersoll during his lifetime and the dwindling number of adherents to the cause even before his death provides an intriguing enigma. As Commager tells it, "Logically, perhaps, [Americans] should have abandoned a religion which, in flagrant contradiction to all experience, taught the depravity of man and the corruption of society . . . but Americans were not a logical people. . . . [I]n everything but law, America at the opening of the twentieth century was a Christian land."[8] Americans were, very simply, *for* religion. And while all the clever ridicule of an Ingersoll could be laughed at, applauded, and even agreed with, it was scarcely enough to dislodge religion from its seat of supremacy.

This is not to say that organized free thought disappeared completely after Ingersoll. The Rationalist Association of North America took up where the American Secular Union had left off, and by 1915, most large cities had their own chapter affiliates.[9] The American Association for the Advancement of Atheism (4-A) received a charter in 1926. But for the most part, the unbelievers were met with less alarm in the twentieth century than they had been before. In fact, the *Literary Digest* of April 1926 reported that the formation of atheist societies in various universities had provoked little concern among the denominations and quoted the *Christian Advocate* (Methodist) as predicting that such societies "may contribute to the intensification of religious zeal and activity." The *Christian Register* (Unitarian) likewise welcomed the societies, saying it was "all for high-spirited and decent controversy," while the secular press gravitated between tolerance and amusement, all the time advocating that such blather be politely ignored.

Such was the state of organized skepticism, then, in the years immediately preceding the issuance of the Humanist Manifesto. In the first three decades of the twentieth century, only H. L. Mencken and Clarence Darrow, among all the unbelievers, attracted national attention, and that was usually for their views on strictly nonreligious matters. Both carried on debates with believers, sometimes, in Darrow's case, with a pathos worthy of an existentialist. "The thing we call 'life,'" he argued, "is nothing other than a state of equilibrium which endures for a short span of years between the two opposing tendencies of nature—the one that builds up and the one that tears down. . . . The energy thus released may be turned into grass or trees . . . but the man— the You and I—is gone—irrevocably dispersed."[10] Such despair was unlikely to reverse the dwindling of the free thinkers' constituency.

One of the interesting distinctions between the advocates of free thought and those of religious humanism is that the former seemed to revel in their jousts with an antiquated faith while the religious humanists, though they shared many of the skeptics' biases, sought to ground their objections to both Christian orthodoxy and modernism in a positive world view. This may, in fact, be one reason religious humanism emerged just at the moment of free thought's decline.

## The Cultural Context: War and Disillusionment

The 1890s was the decade of the social gospel and the progressive movement. Teddy Roosevelt's trust-busting ushered in the new century, and Woodrow Wilson, with his vaunted idealism, would soon be president of the United States. Unbelief was in decline and liberal Christian theology was past its peak, yet the liberal spirit was still thriving throughout the land. No one reflected the mood better than George Santayana, who wrote in 1912,

> The civilization characteristic of Christendom has not disappeared, yet another civilization has begun to take its place. We still understand the value of religious faith. . . . On the other hand the shell of Christendom is broken. . . . Our whole life and mind is saturated with the slow upward filtration of a new spirit—that of an emancipated, atheistic, international democracy.[11]

In short order, however, that new spirit was tragically interrupted by a war in Europe, the heartland of culture. It was in the midst of the postwar social milieu that religious humanism grew up.

The twenties roared with jazz and flappers and booze. The struggle to make the world safe for democracy had made the United States ripe for corpulence. Renewed isolationism abroad was accompanied by the frenetic pursuit of financial aggrandizement at home. "The business of America is business," said President Calvin Coolidge, and it was business that set the tone for the decade. The watchword was *efficiency;* the motive was *profit.* Offering a muckraking view of "our business civilization," James Truslow Adams noted in 1929 that "dealing inevitably with material things . . . tends to locate happiness in them rather than in the intellectual and spiritual." He pronounced the culture without taste or appreciation of the aesthetic, without time for leisure or values.[12]

Post-war Americans yearned for normalcy, and that meant, among other things, that the labor unrest following the end of World War I was answered by the so-called Red scare. President Wilson's attorney general, A. Mitchell Palmer, persecuted resident aliens with lawless raids on their homes and workplaces, ultimately deporting hundreds of them. Hatred and in-group loyalty, so long a part of Americans' war consciousness, dissipated slowly. Radicals, minorities, and dissenters replaced Germans as the objects of middle-American contempt. Reform rabbi and Zionist Stephen Wise, progressive educator John Dewey, and union organizer and socialist Eugene Debs were all considered threats to liberty.

The churches could hardly escape the perversity of reaction. Their "vast promotional campaigns . . . supported the nation's anti-Red hysteria," says Sidney Ahlstrom. "Over and over they depicted religion as a valuable bulwark against radicalism."[13] Clarence True Wilson and his Methodist Board of Prohibition, Temperance, and Public Morals flourished. The clergy prayed for business, and business blessed the church. In New York City, the Swedish Immanuel Congregational Church offered subscribers to its building fund an "engraved certificate of investment in preferred capital stock in the kingdom of God."[14] Bruce Barton's book *The Man Nobody Knows*, published in 1924, nominated Jesus as the "greatest businessman of all time" and promptly became the decade's best-seller. The progressive spirit of the last century was in abeyance; only a few clergy still paid homage to the social gospel. The mainline churches were hardly anxious to do battle with the corporate sins of a society so thoroughly enjoying its return to normalcy. Indeed, as far as the churches were concerned, the formula seemed to be working. Between 1916 and 1926, church membership climbed from 41 million to 54 million persons.[15] Decadence appeared to be paying off.

But statistics fail to measure spirit. Beneath the glitter, something was awry. The simple truths of patriotism had served well during the war, providing direction and purpose. But in the aftermath, life took on new shades of ambiguity and religion lost its certainty. It was not that the average person failed any longer to believe. On the contrary, a 1927 newspaper poll revealed that more than 90 percent of the population believed in God and almost that many believed in the divinity of Jesus.[16] What had changed was not the number of the faithful but the quality or depth of their belief. As Frederick Lewis Allen put it, "There had never been so many books on religious topics in circulation, and the leading divines wrote constantly for the popular magazines; yet all the discussion was itself a sign that religion had become a debatable subject instead of being accepted without question among the traditions of the community."[17]

And why was that? In large part, the answer had to do with the immense prestige attained by the sciences. World War I had thrown into doubt all sorts of traditional assumptions—political, diplomatic, and ethical. Science, however, proved to be the only great intellectual force that had not suffered disrepute. To a great extent, science diminished confidence in Christian formulations and had, indeed, even split the church.

Rural Protestants reacted to Protestant modernism with fear and hostility. It seemed to them that religion was being replaced by physics and sociology, its absolute truth ridiculed or, worse yet, ignored. Small-town and old-stock Americans felt their very ways of life threatened.[18] In 1910, they responded categorically with the booklet *The Fundamentals: A Testimony to the Truth*, detailing five uncompromisable points of doctrine. The fundamentalist-modernist battle was on! And any faith at war with itself was hardly one to inspire.

Beyond that was the socioeconomic reality of the escalating urbanization of the country. The United States in the early twentieth century was fast becoming a nation of metropolises. Between the triumph of science and the chaos of the city, the piety and mystery upon which Christianity had so long depended had been crushed. There had been war, and now there was bustling peace, but there was no sense of harmony, no certainty.

For those sensitive to the confusion, despairing over the fall of liberalism, and disgusted with the wealth and glamour of the reaction that had taken its place, this was truly the age of a "lost generation." Gertrude Stein had first used that label to characterize those expatriate literary and artistic figures who frequented her Paris salon, but it gradually came to apply to all those, many of them young, who turned away from the shallowness of the Anglo-Saxon establishment and sought relief from their discontent in a moral and psychological revolt against main-street mores. F. Scott Fitzgerald put it well in *This Side of Paradise* (1920): "Here was a new generation dedicated more than the last to the fear of poverty and the worship of success, grown up to find all gods dead, all wars fought, all faiths in men shaken." With the end of World War I, the defeat of the League of Nations, and the collapse of President Wilson came the feeling of disillusionment. Those writers who before the war had heralded the coming democratization of culture saw their ideals realized in the person of Warren G. Harding, an incompetent president from the Ohio heartland who presided over one of the most corrupt administrations in history.

Ideas that had nurtured the prewar imagination seemed to have been decimated along with Europe. Socialism, for instance, had been a rallying point, but by the end of the war, the socialist movement had splintered and collapsed.[19] In the light of burgeoning Freudianism, even the human creature, once the darling of the left wing, was now viewed as a mere mechanism, hardly the rational animal Aristotle had once made it out to be. And nothing confirmed the anti-Aristotelian prejudice more, thought these intellectuals, than the debilitating hubbub that was mass America. Sinclair Lewis's novels *Main Street* (1920) and *Babbitt* (1922) symbolized all that was worth detesting.

The response of the "lost generation" to the deterioration they found around them was one of radical doubt and irrationalism. Society was surely beyond redemption. Capitalism was doomed not because it was wrong but because it was political, and politics did not work. Religion was hardly worth a second glance. This was a generation in turmoil, self-absorbed and without perceptible direction. Writing in 1929, Joseph Wood Krutch caught the sentiment of the time. Of human beings in general, he wrote, "[T]here is no reason to suppose that his own life has any more meaning than the humblest insect that crawls from one annihilation to another. Nature . . . has filled . . . the rotting earth with every possible sort of fantastic creature, and among them man is but one—perhaps the most miserable of all, because he is the only one to ask the question, 'Why?'"[20]

This mood could last only so long, however. With the onset of the Great Depression in 1929 came a new interest in radical political and economic thought. Attention focused again on practical social concerns. The malaise of the "lost generation" was replaced by a widespread desire to shed alienation and ennui and to find some ground for a positive, more fruitful approach to living. Social philosopher Lewis Mumford declared in 1931 "that Mr. Krutch should have realized that civilization had merely been molting a dead skin, not going into dissolution." The mood of defeat, Mumford insisted, is dead.[21] And in 1933, the Humanist Manifesto graced the scene.

E. A. Burtt has described religious humanism as a natural development of modernism,[22] and in part, that is true. It is equally astute, however, to view it as a compromise between liberal Christianity and the utter skepticism and note of despair toward things religious represented by the long chain of doubters from Huxley through Ingersoll to the "lost generation" and Krutch. For while religious humanism abandoned the God language of the modernists, it sought to salvage religious sympathies from the throes of a vacant, rock-ribbed materialism. Repudiating the irrationalism and pessimism of the rebellious young, humanism looked to human intelligence and the insights of science to rework the world. Far from seeing the scientific developments of the last half-century as threatening to religion, humanism insisted that they could provide the foundation for a satisfying religious system.

Many of the intellectuals of the late 1920s and early 1930s who were through with the mood of defeat were also dissatisfied with Christianity. They sought a new line of defense against confusion and cosmic threat, a line that would be sophisticated and at the same time supportive of values. They sought a religion that would take science seriously while retaining an ethical framework, that could deal with philosophical and social change and not be straddled with a paralyzing devotion to tradition.

Herbert Schneider has provided an excellent sketch of the myriad people who came together under the banner of religious humanism:

> There are among the humanists left-wing Unitarians who do not reflect the liberalism of Emerson and who do not wish to be confined to Christian limitations. There are materialists who are no longer "doctrinaire" materialists but who are suspicious of theologians who use terms like "soul," "immortal," "transcendental," "God," and "spirit"; they prefer more secular language for their secular truths. There are naturalists who are disgusted by the use of . . . supernatural symbols and myths, . . . who find no use for organized religions, but who have a "religious" concern for the life of reason. There are still a few old-fashioned rationalists, freethinkers or professional atheists. . . . And there are many individuals who cannot be labeled.[23]

No better description of those people who sought a compromise between modernism and nihilism is required. This was the community that was to comprise religious humanism.

# The Emergence of Religious Humanism

Perhaps in no denomination but Unitarianism, with its aversion to creeds and dogma, could such a frankly nontheistic movement as religious humanism have arisen without provoking a schism, and even Unitarianism found itself hard pressed to encompass the new thought. But the denomination had survived theological struggles on this order before; religious humanism was not without its Unitarian forebears.

## Free Religion and the Western Unitarian Conference

Skeptical as it might be about traditional sources of religious authority, early Unitarian transcendentalism was unequivocally Christian. Only that had prevented its adherents from breaking radically with Unitarian orthodoxy during the 1840s and 1850s. With the coming of the Civil War, however, a new brand of transcendentalism appeared, one steeped in the tradition of Theodore Parker's commitment to free inquiry and prepared to follow wherever that inquiry led. In many cases, it led to what might be called *rationalistic theism*. By 1865, a substantial number of young transcendentalists were ready to proclaim their independence from traditional Unitarian Christianity, and soon they would get their chance.

Alarmed at the spread of such radicalism, the National Convention of Unitarian Churches—meeting in New York City in April 1865—adopted a constitutional preamble declaring the delegates' discipleship to the Lord Jesus Christ, a phrase the radicals found eminently unpalatable. When, in October of the following year, the Convention refused to modify its choice of words, the so-called new transcendentalists, led by Francis Ellingwood Abbot and W. J. Potter, met to organize an alternative institution. By May 1867, the Free Religious Association (FRA) had been formed.

Always an amalgamation of theological viewpoints, free religion, as embodied in the FRA, grew slowly for two decades, plagued by its adherents' inability (or unwillingness) to reach a common articulation of its religious posture. In broad terms, it sought the universal element in all religion and grounded that search in a scientific approach to human nature and the external world.

In his "Fifty Affirmations" of free religion, Abbot proclaimed that "the great faith or moving power of free religion is faith in man as a progressive being," and he promoted the goals of brotherhood and universal human cooperation.[1] Unlike traditional Christianity, free religion insisted upon the uniformity of the natural order. According to Stow Persons, it was convinced that "the only method of analysis permissible in the examination of religious and physical phenomena alike was the scientific method."[2] Perfection through education and a fully developed life were the ends the free religionists sought for humankind.

But despite its humanistic overtones, this was still a theistic movement. Abbot called himself a "scientific theist," and Octavius Frothingham—whose little volume, *The Religion of Humanity*, reflected a position that rested on a series of naturalistic assumptions—considered "the interior spirit of any age [to be] the spirit of God," thus identifying God with the life of the mind in history.[3] The FRA represented an attempt by non-Christian positivists to stay within a theistic framework. By the end of the nineteenth century, however, the movement had lost its momentum.

Part of the story of the FRA's demise can be traced to the fact that it chose to strike out on its own and dissociated itself from the institutional base that Unitarianism provided. Nonetheless, the philosophy of free religion made its impact on the larger Unitarian movement, particularly on the Western Unitarian Conference (WUC), that branch of the National Unitarian Conference formed in 1852 to promote the faith west of New York State.

In 1875, the WUC found itself at odds with eastern orthodoxy over many of the same issues raised by the FRA and consequently hired its own missionary secretary, Jenkin Lloyd Jones, to oversee the organization of churches from the Appalachians to the Rockies. The WUC, said the Conference, "conditions its fellowship on no dogmatic tests but welcomes all thereto who wish to work with it in advancing the Kingdom of God."[4] Following that invitation to the letter, Jones encouraged the spread of all varieties of liberalism and was more than sympathetic to a scientifically respectable faith. His ideal church, he said, would be "the thinker's home." Moreover, "The student of science will handle no discoveries that it will not prize and indulge in no guesses that it will not respect."[5]

Scientific theism and its intellectual purveyors gradually spread throughout the Unitarian West until the more orthodox Unitarians were prompted to respond via Jones's successor, Jabez Sunderland. During the 1886 WUC annual meeting, Sunderland pinpointed the issue by asking, "Is Western Unitarianism ready to give up its Christian theistic character?" Declaring that a "united, purposive, determined group of men . . . want to remove Unitarianism off its historic base to Free or Ethical Religion,"[6] Sunderland and his followers warned that the WUC was slipping dangerously far from Unitarianism's age-old commitment to "God and worship, to the idea of divine humanity that shines in Christ Jesus." They would do all they could to draw it back.

But the majority of the WUC would not follow. Instead, the Conference adopted a resolution reaffirming that its fellowship was conditioned on no dogmatic tests but open to all who struggled for truth, righteousness, and love. The defeat stunned the conservative party, who withdrew in a matter of weeks to form the Western Unitarian Association (WUA). Not even the stirring words of William Channing Gannett's "Things Commonly Believed among Us" (delivered to the 1887 annual meeting of the WUC), which affirmed "the growing nobility of Man" and urged the worship and love of God, could entice the orthodox diehards back. It was not until 1894 (the Reconciliation of Saratoga) that unity of sorts was reestablished on the western front.

The religious humanists of the 1920s were not unaware of the theological struggles of the nineteenth century. The western issue had crystallized Unitarian creedlessness, and if it had not offered an explicitly nontheistic stance, it had encouraged intellectual exploration to whatever ends truth and science led. In the appreciative words of Raymond B. Bragg (who wrote his Bachelor of Divinity thesis on the FRA), free religion and the WUC had "shifted the perspective of religion from the clouds to the human scene."[7] Twentieth-century Unitarian humanism would self-consciously see itself as a natural development of free religion and would, in no small part, owe a debt to the FRA and the WUC for its home in the denomination.

Nonetheless, the majority of Unitarians in the 1920s were hardly more sympathetic to a nontheistic philosophy than Sunderland and his

orthodox associates had been to free religion. Religious humanism was
forced to struggle, to do battle for its very existence. It was staunchly
opposed, even ridiculed by its theistic Unitarian opponents. But in a surprisingly short time, it would establish itself as a fully reputable option
within the Unitarian fold.

## The Rise of Early Religious Humanism

The early period of religious humanism may be said to date from the
meeting of John Dietrich and Curtis W. Reese at the 1917 session of
the WUC in Des Moines through the election in 1937 of Frederick
May Eliot as president of the American Unitarian Association (AUA).[8]
Although Eliot was not a doctrinaire humanist, he had contributed to
Reese's book *Humanist Sermons* and, as chair of the 1934 AUA Commis-
sion on Appraisal, had sympathetically recognized humanism's aversion
to theology and traditional religious language. Eliot was considered an
ally, if not a devotee, of the humanist cause, and his nomination
prompted a revolt among some theists who nominated their own candidate, Rev. Charles R. Joy. Before the election, however, with sentiment
in the denomination running strongly against another divisive theological battle, Joy was persuaded to withdraw and Eliot was elected without
opposition.[9] Thus, Eliot's election may be seen, at least symbolically, as a
radical lessening of antipathy toward humanism and a grudging recognition within more conservative Unitarian circles that it had earned its
place and was here to stay.

In attempting to date the period of early religious humanism, however, it is important to note two points. First, the humanist impulse
simmered long before the twentieth century. And second, in some sense,
it was the publication of the Humanist Manifesto in 1933, not Eliot's
election, that marked the climax of religious humanism's early growth.
Instead of coming at the beginning of the movement and serving as a
call to arms or herald of the new faith, the Humanist Manifesto seems to
have come toward the plateau and acted more as a mechanism of consolidation. Humanism grew steadily—in membership, sympathy, and
spirit—from the days of the 1921 Unitarian National Conference in
Detroit through the 1933 publication of the Humanist Manifesto.
Shortly thereafter, however, the *New Humanist* ceased publication, the
controversies subsided, and, particularly with the coming of World War
II, religious humanism as a movement separate from Unitarianism
started to fade.

Perhaps the first Unitarian minister to use the term *humanism* was Frank C. Doan of Meadville Theological School, then located in Meadville, Pennsylvania. Professor of psychology and philosophy of religion, Doan was a disciple of both William James and F. C. S. Schiller[10] and introduced a philosophy he dubbed *cosmic humanism* to the American Philosophical Association in 1908. Doan's thought was, in fact, much closer to modernism than to humanism,[11] but the philosopher always insisted upon starting with the human in his search for the divine.[12]

Doan's humanism had a profound impact on three Meadville students, each of whom would play a significant role in the development of religious humanism: J. A. C. Fagginner Auer, later a leading humanist church history scholar at Harvard Divinity School and author of the popular *Humanism States Its Case*;[13] Charles H. Lyttle, who would later serve as church history professor at Meadville and influence a younger generation of humanists; and E. Burdette Backus, who would become a distinguished humanist minister in Los Angeles and Indianapolis. Both Auer and Backus were signers of the Humanist Manifesto. Regardless of the name of his philosophy, however, Doan was a liberal theist, and religious humanism represented a movement beyond liberal theism. We must look, therefore, to Dietrich and Reese to find the formal beginnings of religious humanism within Unitarianism.

Neither Dietrich nor Reese came to Unitarianism the easy way. Dietrich had been ordained a minister in the Reformed Church, but he was charged with heresy in 1911 on the grounds that he denied the infallibility of the Bible, the virgin birth, the deity of Jesus, and the efficacy of atonement. Although unafraid to confront his accusers in a formal trial, the young minister decided that such a public spectacle would accomplish little and therefore resigned from the Reformed ministry. Within a matter of months, he was accepted into fellowship with the American Unitarian Association and settled in the First Unitarian Society of Spokane, Washington.[14]

Reese had covered even more spiritual distance on his journey to liberalism. Raised in a rigidly orthodox family in the Blue Ridge Mountains of North Carolina, he had, perhaps not surprisingly, chosen the Southern Baptist ministry as his vocation. But exposure to biblical criticism in seminary nurtured a series of doubts that remained unabated throughout his first pastorate in a liberal Baptist church in Ohio. "I could and did say what I believed," Reese recalled, "but I did not feel free to reveal what I did not believe,"[15] which included the infallibility of the

Bible, the virgin birth, redemption through Christ, and eternal damnation. Eventually, Reese could stand the cognitive dissonance no longer and, impressed by the social gospel of Francis Greenwood Peabody, explored the possibility of entering the Unitarian ministry. Upon hearing of his conversion to the liberal church, Reese's mother announced that she would rather have seen him dead, for at least then he would have been walking with the angels![16]

## John Dietrich

Even though by 1913 Dietrich and Reese had both found Unitarianism, they had not yet declared themselves humanists. It was three years later, during the last year of his Spokane ministry, that Dietrich announced that he was a humanist. Biographer Carleton Winston describes Dietrich's discovery of the term:

> Though long familiar with the humanism of the Renaissance, Dietrich came across the word "humanism" in a different connotation through an article by Frederick M. Gould in the London magazine published by the British Ethical Societies. Gould, an ardent advocate of August Comte and his Positivism, . . . used the word "Humanism" in the sense of the belief and trust in human effort. And it struck a responsive note in Dietrich. . . . [T]his . . . would be a good name for his interpretation of religion in contrast to theism.[17]

On November 1, 1916, Dietrich took his brand of humanism to the ministry of the First Unitarian Society of Minneapolis, where it was to grow and flourish until his retirement in 1936. Dietrich's Minneapolis ministry was one of the great Unitarian ministries of the twentieth century in terms of its breadth and influence. Largely inattentive to the pastoral dimension of his calling (he was quoted as saying, "In my ministry people have to have the courage to work through their personal problems by themselves"[18]), Dietrich devoted the bulk of his time and energy to the preparation of long, meticulous sermons. These were his principal vehicles for propagating the humanist gospel, for he wrote no nationally published books. At times, as many as two thousand people would crowd the Garrick Theater to hear the minister's Sunday address, and many thousands more would tune into its radio broadcast. The service itself was simple: some readings, music, a statement of aspiration, and then an hour-long address.

Dietrich's name and the details of his new religion spread quickly, thanks to the publication of his sermons in collected form[19] and to the recognition accorded him by such writers as Harry Elmer Barnes, who said of Dietrich's humanism, "It . . . [is] the most sincere, intelligent, consistent, and promising effort . . . [to harmonize] . . . the religious impulse with the . . . facts of modern knowledge."[20]

And exactly what was this new humanism the ex-Reformed minister espoused? In the first place, it was a faith beyond modernism. Dietrich was convinced that the modernists' attempt to revitalize ancient terminology was bound to fail. "There is just a word I would speak to . . . every Modernist," he said. "[S]uch terms and phrases as you use are more confusing than clarifying. They show an attempt to mix modern scientific thought with ancient theology. It cannot be done."[21]

At the same time that he rejected liberal Christianity, however, Dietrich also shied away from the Bertrand Russell–Joseph Wood Krutch brand of what he referred to as *futilitarianism*. He refused to concede that humans were alienated from nature or that the universe was unfriendly to human projects. The first presupposition of his faith— what he often called "the greatest discovery of the ages"—was that the universe was governed by law and not caprice. Dietrich was convinced that by understanding and acting in accordance with those laws, human beings could better their situations. Of the futilitarians, Dietrich remarked, "The mistake all these critics make is in separating man from nature and looking upon nature as antagonistic to man's purposes and ideals. . . . We are not alien creatures in a strange land. . . . We are . . .the natural development of its forces and conditions."[22]

But Dietrich's naturalism was hardly mechanistic. Indeed, a central pillar of his philosophy was a faith in cosmic power as a transformative agent in the universe:

> The universe is growing to be something better, something higher, something finer, year by year. . . . It is a manifestation of a power that is resistless, that is working in accordance with law which is perfect and invariable, and which is constantly seeking higher levels. In other words, we may be sure that there is in the universe a cosmic power which expresses itself in a law of progress.[23]

Generally unwilling to attach the label *God* to this phenomenon, Dietrich acknowledged that historically, most religions had focused upon a God concept. He argued, however, that an examination of the anthropological or biological roots of religion, rather than its forms, would reveal "something deeper than these forms . . . an urge within man himself toward better adjustment, toward a fuller and freer life."[24] There was no need to use theistic terminology.

Although Dietrich would not speak generally of God (he did occasionally refer sympathetically to the "god of evolution," "an immanent force pervading the whole universe"[25]), neither would he deny God altogether. He described his attitude toward God in this fashion: "[I]t is that of inquiry. I am entirely open-minded and not dogmatic toward the idea of God. But while I do not call myself an atheist, neither do I call myself a theist. . . . I do not deny such [guiding] intelligence [as in theism]. I simply see no evidence of it."[26] Dietrich preached that our religious attention would best be directed not at God but at those capacities and means that we possess to change the world. He strongly believed that education and an ethical system grounded in the natural world of human need might be effective agents for the creation of the abundant life:

> [T]hrough a knowledge of [the universe's] constant ways, man can wrench from it everything he deems worthwhile. . . . Nature . . . is but clay which he can mold into the house of his dreams. . . . And what he does to nature he can also do to human nature. He can discover the laws of his own being and his social environment and eventually control those to his own advantage.[27]

Dietrich manifested humanism's classic overestimation of the human capacity to subdue nature. It was exactly this kind of sentiment that prepared the way for the decline of humanism, outside of Unitarianism, in the wake of the Great Depression and a second disastrous world war.

Dietrich was prepared to admit, however, that there was one human limitation that could not be overcome, and that was death. Death should be met with courage and forthrightness and accepted as an integral part of the natural process. Tragedies, said Dietrich, "should be endured in such a way that they leave us better and not worse as a result of our experience. If we would live at all, we must be able to look trouble and suffering in the face and cope with it in a manly way."[28]

This, in sum, is Rev. John Dietrich's religious thought. It is startling to note how much of it is carried virtually full blown into the Humanist Manifesto: the rejection of modernism; the grounding of humanity in naturalistic and evolutionary processes; the understanding of religion as "an urge . . .toward a fuller . . . life"; the reverence toward science and the confidence in human intelligence; the conviction that human beings can mold nature to their own ends; and the antitragic, unsentimental, "manly" attitude toward limitation. Certainly, additions and expansions to the Manifesto would come later, but the basic framework was there. Dietrich was the first and greatest of a series of popularizers of a movement that soon would claim some of the most sophisticated minds in the United States. Appropriately enough, he has been called "the father of religious humanism."[29]

## Curtis W. Reese

The cofounder of religious humanism, Curtis Reese, began his Unitarian ministry at a small church in Alton, Illinois, but assumed the pulpit of the First Unitarian Church in Des Moines, Iowa, in 1915. During his second year in Des Moines, Reese preached what he described as "the first systematically Humanist sermon preached from any pulpit in America."[30] Presumably, he is referring to his well-known address "A Democratic View of Religion," which he distributed to delegates at the 1917 WUC meeting in his city and which served as the basis for his conversation with Dietrich at that same meeting. In this groundbreaking sermon, Reese said that the democratic view of religion stood in contrast to the theocratic or autocratic. In the latter, the will of the autocrat was done; in the former, human will and action were what mattered. A democratic religion "holds that this is man's world and that it largely depends on man what the world order shall be like." Reese went on to emphasize the importance of the scientific method to solve problems and the need to reorient religious thought from preoccupation with God's glory to the achievement of human welfare.[31]

Reese left Des Moines, and thus the preaching ministry, in 1919 to become secretary of the WUC, a largely administrative position, which he held until 1930, when he was appointed dean of the Abraham Lincoln Center, a social service center in Chicago. The details of his religious thinking therefore are not recorded in sermon form (as they are in Dietrich's case) but rather in four books that he authored or edited: *Humanism* (1926); *Humanist Sermons* (1927); *Humanist Religion* (1931); and *The Meaning of Humanism* (1945). The first three, in particular, had a profound impact upon the fledgling movement and were considered for many years the standard resources for a capsulized understanding of humanist thought.

Like Dietrich, Reese rejected both modernism and what he referred to as "the old materialism." Of the latter, he said that it had no room for novelty and refused to take mind and personality seriously enough. Instead, Reese took what might be best described as an *organicist* position, which saw the human creature developing toward some end and for some purpose that evolutionary processes made possible. Philosophy professor Mason Olds summarizes Reese's perspective in these terms: "Although man is continuous with nature, in him the organic rises to 'mental levels.' . . . [T]he organism becomes conscious of its purpose; namely, to direct the process so that man's life might be enhanced. . . . [B]y learning how the processes work, man can become a participant in the creative processes."[32]

Science was the primary tool for ascertaining information about those processes, and in conjunction with intelligence, it could provide guidelines and mechanisms for democratizing human conduct and remaking the world. Reese outlined the procedure as follows: "Intelligence applied to any given problem involves . . . the collation of . . . facts, . . . understanding of a goal that is both desirable and possible, . . . and . . . the technical skill to enlist and direct all available forces in the achievement of the desired goal. This is human engineering."[33]

Reese thought that religion should be involved in the process of formulating these goals, and he recommended a kind of experimental democracy in which various plans and values were attempted but always with the understanding that they could be changed if they failed.[34] The principle underlying all faith and action had to be that it led to the creation of a more rewarding life for human beings. Thus, Reese described religion as "a human effort to find satisfactory models of living, in the course of which many . . . theories may be postulated, tested, and abandoned; the abiding thing being the urge to newer and newer efforts to reach ever receding goals."[35]

Perhaps more specifically and concretely than any other humanist, Reese was willing to elaborate social goals and policies that would help realize the ends toward which his religion strove.[36] Many of Reese's views are similar to Dietrich's. Nonetheless, the Humanist Manifesto reflects pointedly Reesian sentiments when, in the seventh point, it defines religion as "all that is in its degree expressive of intelligently satisfying living," and, in the eighth point, sets the religious goal of "the complete realization of human personality," which simultaneously accounts for and requires "social passion."

Finally, it was Reese, among others, who introduced the element of philosophical pragmatism to humanism. Whereas Dietrich was, in many ways, a devotee of University of Michigan philosopher Roy Wood Sellars's critical realism (and evolutionary naturalism), Reese was fascinated by the possibilities of an applied experimentalism along the lines of John Dewey's thinking at Columbia University.[37] Dietrich and Reese represent the slightly divergent emphases that come together and are reflected in religious humanism and the Manifesto: Sellarian realism and Deweyan instrumentalism. (See Appendix B.)

The final issue is whether Reese's was a religion without God. More reluctant than Dietrich and others to discard the term *God*, Reese distinguished between theism (as an elaborate system of beliefs about God) and a simple belief in some kind of divinity (probably approaching a concept of evolutionary process).[38] Toward the latter, he adopted a sympathetic stance and, in general, took an inquisitive, open-minded approach to deity.

## First Signs of Controversy

With the discovery by Dietrich and Reese at the 1917 WUC meeting that they both held to and preached a humanistic faith, Unitarian religious humanism as a formal movement felt its birth pangs. Yet the years immediately following that historic meeting were devoid of further national development of the movement, in large part because both the denomination and the world were preoccupied with World War I. What religious energy most Americans could muster was absorbed by President Woodrow Wilson's plea to join a crusade destined to make the world safe for democracy. Dietrich and Reese were content to preach their newfound philosophy to their respective congregations. And in due time, their position would make its impact upon the larger (and more conservative) wing of the denomination.

With the termination of the war, the populace could once more direct its attention to metaphysical issues. The post-war cynicism, self-doubt, and reaction seemed to Dietrich and Reese to require a renewed faith in human possibilities. The introduction of the new humanism on the denominational level came in March 1919 with the publication of Dietrich's essay "The Religion of Experience" on the front page of the Unitarian magazine the *Christian Register*. In a few lines, Dietrich sought to distinguish between supernatural religion and a faith that "looks for no help or consolation from without, . . . where no help comes, [but turns people's attention] to a firm and confident reliance upon themselves, in whom lie the possibilities of all things."[39] Here, in germinal form, was religious humanism.[40]

The response to Dietrich's essay was fast in coming. Letters to the editor, most of them critical, filled the pages of the *Register* for almost three months. Editor Albert C. Dieffenbach encouraged the dialogue, acknowledging that Dietrich represented the views of many Unitarians, particularly in the western United States. Indeed, the critical and positive letters could almost be divided by geographical location: the former coming predominantly from New England and the latter from Erie, Pennsylvania, and points west. One of those who applauded Dietrich and added his personal testimony to humanism's promotion was a young minister by the name of E. Burdette Backus, a subsequent a signer of the Manifesto. Said Backus, "I can bear testimony from my own heart that it [humanism] does bring me satisfactions and power that are simply unavailable under the old forms of thought."[41]

The controversy surrounding Dietrich's article abated by summer 1919, and it was a year before the issue of humanism was again raised in the pages of the *Register*. In the interim, Reese had resigned his Des Moines ministry to become secretary of the WUC, and it was his address in July 1920, to the Cambridge Summer School for Ministers at Harvard University, that sparked the next tempest over the new faith.

Entitled "The Content of Religious Liberalism," this address was intended to be a statement of what Reese thought to be the common understanding of Unitarianism, at least as he had experienced it in the WUC. He was, therefore, stunned at the fury of the response of his eastern colleagues to his proclamation that although liberalism needed to remain open to future scientific discoveries about God, it was "building a religion that would not be shaken even if the old thought of God were outgrown." Reese went on to state his conviction that "purposive and powerful cosmic processes were operative" in the universe (regardless of whether one called them *God*) and that for liberals in religion, the "*contemplation* of cosmic events has given way to *regulated observation of and experiment* with cosmic processes; and this has led to conscious cooperation with and partial control [of them]."[42]

But Reese's naturalistic conceptions of process were not good enough for most of those in attendance at the Harvard summer school. Following Reese's presentation, Dr. William G. Eliot, then minister of the First Unitarian Church of Portland, Oregon, arose to declare, with voice atremble, "I would suffer my right arm to be severed from my body before I would take God from my people!"[43] Several ministers—most notably Samuel McChord Crothers of Cambridge, Massachusetts, and John Lathrop of Brooklyn, New York—defended Reese's right to speak as he did, although they could not support the substance of his address. But the bulk of those assembled were outraged. Describing the affair some forty years later, Reese wrote in a somewhat sarcastic vein,

> The earlier Western issue [involving free religion in the West[44]] was fought over the freedom of the pew. Now, some forty years later, I was carrying the battle from the pew to the pulpit. And people were never too much concerned about what the pew believed . . . but were horror-stricken over the prospect of ministers who did not put any limits to the freedom of the pulpit.
>
> The early Western Conference . . . men did not especially question the Judaic-Christian tradition nor did they at all question the theistic basis of religion. But in my Harvard Summer School address I [did both]. . . . This was simply too much for the tender-minded Unitarian clergy to take. . . . One gentle soul put his right hand on my left shoulder and said in bated breath, "I am sorry for you."[45]

Others, however, welcomed the discussion Reese had stimulated. Albert Dieffenbach, editor of the *Christian Register*, for example, commented that "some of us have not grown an inch in fifty years." But Dieffenbach was still unable to allow that the humanists were dismissing anything more than the word *God*. What Reese advocated, he wrote, was for followers to place "less responsibility up to God than [they] once did, and more obligation down to [their] own self-dependent minds and wills."[46] Be that as it may, Reese's comments resulted in greater publicity than ever for the new faith.

One other event of some significance occurred in the summer of 1920. Upon Reese's suggestion, the *Christian Register* asked Rev. Sidney S. Robins of Ann Arbor, Michigan, to seek out Professor Roy Wood Sellars for an interview; the subsequent article, "What Is a Humanist? This Will Tell You," was published in the July 29 edition of the magazine, just a few days after Reese had delivered his Harvard summer school address. Sellars had been an influential figure with both Dietrich and Reese, and his book *The Next Step in Religion* (1918) had been one of the first attempts by a nonclergyperson to articulate a humanist faith. A well-respected philosopher at the University of Michigan, Sellars was one of the originators of a new epistemology that he initially dubbed *critical realism*, but his interests were broad, stretching from cosmology to politics to religion. A long-time Unitarian, Sellars would exert a continuing and powerful influence upon the entire humanist movement.

Sellars's first statement in a Unitarian journal was hardly a systematic presentation of his position or even a thorough answer to the article's title question, but it added the weight of the philosopher's prestige to the growing conflict. Immediately rejecting supernaturalism, Sellars urged the church to turn to a contemplation of what creates human happiness. Many of the issues religion had presumed to deal with authoritatively, he opined, were, in fact, matters of utter speculation. He also thought ministers should acknowledge that they have no special insight; they should seek simply to stimulate discussion of the "deeper problems of life."[47] Interestingly enough, the scholarly Sellars suggested that too much emphasis had been placed upon rationality in Unitarian circles.

"The two elements to be added to the intellect are the aesthetic and the social," Sidney Robins quoted the professor as saying. "The new religion must develop a ritual of its own, or a certain orderliness or beauty of its own."[48] (Since Sellars penned the first draft of the Humanist Manifesto, the entire document bears his imprint; its concern with the social dimension, therefore, no doubt reflects the philosopher's own concerns, as expressed even as early as 1920. Perhaps it is startling, given Sellars's comments here, that except indirectly in the twelfth point, very little is said of the aesthetic dimension in the Manifesto.)

The response to Sellars, as it had been to Dietrich and Reese, was vociferous. "A gentleman in Washington, D.C. . . . ," Dieffenbach wrote two weeks later, "says for such religion [as Sellars's] he would not give a dime and we ought not to have given an interview on this line in a Unitarian paper. We are in duty bound to teach God!" Once again, the editor insisted that the humanists were not explicitly denying God and that, in any case, their viewpoint needed to be heard.[49]

A distinguished parish minister (Dietrich), a well-known denominational official (Reese), and a respected professional philosopher (Sellars) had all now publicly identified themselves with humanism. The stage was set for confrontation. That encounter would come in October 1921.

## The Detroit Conference

Reese's elevation to an administrative post within the Unitarian organization put him in a convenient position to promote the humanist cause. Perhaps his most critical intervention came when he invited Dietrich to address the 1921 annual meeting of the WUC on "The Outlook for

Religion." This speech set in motion a chain of events climaxed by a historic debate later that year at the Unitarian National Conference meeting in Detroit.

Dietrich's address to the WUC in Chicago on May 16, 1921, was a straightforward presentation of his longtime conviction that if religion was to survive, it must accommodate itself to modern thought, and that if it did so, it would be natural, not supernatural, and humanistic, not theistic.[50] Even though there was nothing new here, as far as Dietrich's philosophy was concerned, the address drew a fervent objection from Rev. George R. Dodson, minister of Unity Church in St. Louis, Missouri, and professor of philosophy at Washington University. Dodson reproached Reese for allowing a person of Dietrich's views to appear on a Unitarian platform, thus giving the impression that his words were representative of Unitarian thought. Reese, who had been subjected to similar attacks the previous summer at Harvard, defended the appropriateness of Dietrich's presence and reminded Dodson that if Unitarianism stood for nothing else, it stood for freedom of expression.[51]

Dodson was not, however, to be dissuaded, and in the August 11, 1921, edition of the *Christian Register,* he published a short article, "Clear Thinking or Death," that stoked the national fires again. Castigating the notion that Unitarianism stood merely for liberty, Dodson insisted that it had always implicitly affirmed a common faith in God. But now, he said, some ministers were preaching atheistic humanism and, in obvious references to Dietrich and Reese, he wrote,

> A speaker in the Western Conference in May declared . . . that the thought of God will have to go, that the long evolution of the idea of God is to end in no idea at all, and that the future belongs to an atheistic humanism. . . . When a protest was made to the Western Secretary, . . . he defended his action [of inviting the speaker].
>
> Consider what this means. A man whose business is largely that of securing ministers for churches repeatedly states that he does not consider theism essential, but is satisfied with men who preach atheistic humanism.[52]

Dodson went on to predict that such atheism would lead to the death of the denomination. He argued that "we must avow our faith in God, even though the statement of that faith may remind us of a creed."[53] This article was one of the first full-blown theistic attacks upon the new faith.

Dodson was fast emerging as a principal spokesperson for theism, and in the following issue of the *Register*, he was joined by another critic of humanism, Rev. William L. Sullivan, a former preceptor at the College of the Paulist Fathers in Georgetown, who had left Roman Catholicism and joined Unitarianism because "he refused to sign the anti-modernist oath imposed by Pius X upon all Catholic teachers in 1907."[54] Minister of the staid All Souls Church in New York City, Sullivan was identified with the more conservative elements in the denomination and sought in his *Register* article, entitled "God, No-God, Half-God," to discredit the "no-Goddites" and, even more, believers in what he called "Half-God," or God as evolutionary process, as One who "blunders and flounders and experimentally struggles." In direct reference to Reese, Sullivan lambasted the notion of a "democratic God" and asserted that only an infinitely powerful, sure-footed God would do.[55] Although there is no evidence of planned collaboration between Dodson and Sullivan at this point, it is clear that their two essays, coming in back-to-back issues of the national magazine, propelled the conflict into even wider view.

Dodson's essay had two immediate consequences. The first was an offer by Dietrich, who had been scheduled to address the annual Unitarian National Conference meeting in Detroit that October, to withdraw if his views were not considered sufficiently representative of Unitarian thought. Palfrey Perkins, secretary of the Conference, refused Dietrich's offer, but the program committee did decide to ask Sullivan to join Dietrich on the platform.[56] The second consequence of the Dodson article was a renewal in even more spirited terms of the previous years' debates in the pages of the *Register*. Following publication of Dodson's "Clear Thinking or Death," six articles, twenty-four letters, and several editorials were devoted to the debate. By the time the Conference met in October, the delegates had been well exposed to the issue and were looking forward to a heated exchange. They were not to be disappointed.

A review of this correspondence in the *Register* reveals several things of interest. In the first place, the contenders were no longer divided geographically, as they had been in the 1919 dispute over Dietrich's article. New England ministers now joined in the substantive defense of humanism, and letter writers from the West supported Dodson (who was, after all, from St. Louis). In the second place, not all the writers were yet clear (as even the humanists were not) as to whether humanism required a denial of God. For example, writing for the *Register* in defense of the new faith, distinguished scholar Richard W. Boynton argued that humanism was simply developing a "more pragmatic . . . idea of God" and that the charge of atheism, which was always leveled at those who disagreed with one's views, was utterly misplaced.[57] In a letter of reply to his critics, Dodson corrected Boynton and others and insisted, "We were told at Chicago that theism itself must be given up, that it belongs to the past. . . . I understand it to mean the rejection of all conceptions of God whatsoever."[58]

Reese took issue with Dodson's unequivocal identification of theism as the only legitimate system of God belief. "If by atheism is meant the denial of a power greater than one's self," he wrote, "there are no atheists," and he went on to point out that theism (in the sense of belief in an anthropomorphic being) was "a respectable philosophical hypothesis—nothing more." Reese claimed that religion could survive, even flourish, without God, and he closed with his famous declaration, "Theism is philosophically possible, but not religiously necessary." Reese's reluctance to give up God altogether (which is typical of this first generation of humanists) is reflected in this famous letter. In addition to the metaphysical issue, he addressed himself to the criticism of having encouraged humanist ministers: "It is out of the question to require men to commit themselves on highly controversial technical metaphysical problems before commending them to churches or inviting them to address a conference."[59]

Besides Reese, no other signers of the Manifesto participated in this printed dialogue. But Doan, the old "cosmic humanist," then minister in Iowa City, did contribute a letter taking Dodson to task for his disparagement of liberty![60]

In response to his critics, Dodson reiterated his conviction that the Conference ought to issue a statement of consensus, not of "what Unitarians must believe, but . . . of what they generally do believe,"[61] and he and Sullivan hoped to see such a litany endorsed by the meeting. The evening of Wednesday, October 5, 1921, drew near, therefore, amid an atmosphere of expectation and tension. This was to be the first head-on encounter before the entire denomination by the leading spokespersons for the two positions.

Rev. Dilworth Lupton of Cleveland preceded the two major speakers with a simple confessional statement of theism.[62] But it was Dietrich and Sullivan the large audience in the Temple Beth-El had come to hear, and Dietrich was the next to address the gathering. Modern people had come to realize, he proclaimed, that no ecclesiastical religion and no

God beyond humanity would assist them in creating the Kingdom of God on earth. The building of the perfect society, though it may never be realized in an individual's lifetime, is solely a human task; it would involve no divine intervention, no miracle working from God. "The kind of world we live in," said Dietrich, "depends not upon some God outside of man, but upon man himself, or, as some of us would put it, upon the God that dwells in humanity. . . . [W]e must insist that whatever God does, he does through men and not for them."63

As a straightforward statement of humanism, Dietrich's speech was really quite moderate in that he made room for the concept of God, albeit a modified one, and did not refer to his faith as *humanist* but as *Unitarian*. In addition, he not only repudiated an anthropomorphic, interventionist God but also rejected "some supreme cosmic principle that is working inevitably along the lines of progress toward the better era, regardless of what man does or fails to do."64 Dietrich was differentiating between the new religious humanists and many of the early evolutionary philosophers, both Christian and nontheist, who put trust in blind, constructive evolutionary impulses to build a better order. Dietrich, Reese, and their associates were clearly aligned with the Huxleyan tradition: Cosmic processes had to be supplemented by intelligent cooperation if they were to be turned to human benefit; a *laissez-faire* attitude was not enough.65 Dietrich's expression of the humanist position was met with enthusiasm by his fellow humanists at the Conference and by those who still took seriously the ideals of the social gospel.

Next, Sullivan arose to make the case for theism, and in impassioned tones, he ripped into those who thought no individual could speak for Unitarianism and proceeded to construct a fairly elaborate argument for God from moral law. Unitarians, he said, had always believed "that man is under a law which he has got to obey because of its divineness and that the moral of this law . . . is conscience within his soul." Of course, the source of this moral law was the Heart of the Universe, the Soul of Being, God, and he or she who would ignore this fact betrayed a "cowardly spirit."66

It was not the intellectual substance of Sullivan's address but rather his tone and demeanor toward the humanists that turned the assembly's sympathies to Dietrich. Because Sullivan believed so fanatically in the danger of a nontheistic view, he began to mock the humanists, asking, for instance, whether their God could be a "bundle of gas" and declaring that without an appreciation of the true God's moral law, we would be reduced to amateur speeches about democracy and dilettantish comments about the social order—obvious swipes at Reese. Finally, Sullivan implied that if one had lost the faith he spoke of, the only alternative of integrity was to leave the church. He concluded with the words, "God will not be mocked!"[67]

Many of the delegates, the majority of whom agreed with Sullivan's theological position, were offended by the personal nature of his attack, and thereby rendered unreceptive to the confessional statement that Dodson and Sullivan had intended to introduce. The two ministers, sensing that their cause had been lost, decided against even bringing the matter before the Conference. Not all the delegates were turned off by Sullivan's approach, of course, and a drive to draft him as Laymen's League Missionary at Large was begun the night of his speech. Nevertheless, from the theists' point of view, it was unfortunate that Dodson had not been chosen to represent their faith, for that very afternoon he had "spoken for theism" to the ministers' luncheon and had done so with humor and without bile.[68]

Humanism had won a great victory in Detroit—not in terms of gaining converts to its thinking but in terms of the national denomination's refusal to pass any kind of statement that would banish humanists from the church. There would be no repeat performance of the 1857 Syracuse Convention, which had resulted in the eventual formation of the Free Religious Association. The Unitarian Church was still one.

## A Decade of Growth

The years 1922 to 1933 constituted a unique period of growth for religious humanism, both within Unitarianism and gradually throughout certain segments of the intellectual world. Humanism caught the spirit of the times among the left-wing religious; with new converts, new publications, and new institutions, it was coming into its own. Among the reasons for its emergence were the conversion to humanism of many ministers and churches; the renewal of the controversy in the *Christian Register*; the coming of a new generation of humanists, particularly out of Meadville Theological School in Chicago; the influence of A. Eustace Haydon; the founding of the *New Humanist* magazine; the conflict over theism as "humanism plus"; the break with Unitarianism and the founding of independent humanist societies by Charles Francis Potter and others; and the flurry of important books issued between 1926 and 1930. All these events led up to the writing of the Humanist Manifesto in 1933.

The years immediately following the National Unitarian Conference in Detroit (1921–1926) were relatively quiet ones for humanism. Surprisingly, no pertinent letters appeared in the *Register* in the weeks following the Dietrich-Sullivan confrontation. Perhaps the denomination had temporarily tired of the business, or perhaps the failure to defeat humanism in Detroit had temporarily stifled theism. Having been exposed to humanism, more and more Unitarian ministers and churches took up the banner throughout the 1920s. Writing in 1927 of these early years, John Dietrich observed,

> First there was a sympathetic attitude on the part of several ministers, and this eventually changed to conversion. Time and time again we would hear that this or that minister had become a humanist. One of the most important accessions to the humanist ranks was Dr. A. Wakefield Slaten. Only five years ago [1922] Dr. Slaten was teaching in a Baptist college . . . [and was] ousted for heretical views. He came into Unitarian fellowship and in a couple of years had become an out and out humanist. . . . [H]e is a man of unusual ability . . . and occupies a strategic point in the West Side church in New York.[69]

In 1925, A. Wakefield Slaten succeeded Charles Francis Potter (who was soon to become a leading humanist himself) as minister of the prestigious West Side Unitarian Church in New York City, and from the beginning of his ministry there, he projected a decidedly humanist tone. In an early sermon, with obvious (though uncredited) reference to Roy Wood Sellars, Slaten remarked, "The next step in religion [is] . . . the wholehearted and unreserved acceptance of the naturalistic . . . point of view."[70] Slaten went on to proclaim human beings as "evolution's highest product."[71]

Slaten's sermons are interesting because they embody some of what we might call humanism's greatest weaknesses while appearing to move a step beyond popular humanist thought of the day. His uncritical optimism, for instance, is typical of the buoyant prophecies rampant in the 1920s: "[A] better race is in prospect," he said on October 17, 1926. "[N]ever has there been such an opportunity for sublime living as we now possess. . . . The soul of humanity is becoming nobler."[72] Another decade would dampen that joy, however. In fact, it was exactly that kind of unrestrained optimism that the neo-orthodox would find so contemptible about humanism and that a thinker such as James Luther Adams would eventually try to counteract.

Slaten's comments on nature provide another example of early humanism's excesses—in this case, its insistence that nature is a tool set at humanity's disposal. The job of humanity, he said, "is the conquest of this planet as a habitation for man, the discovery and utilization of Nature's boundless powers."[73]

If Slaten was guilty of common humanist errors, then he was also cognizant of some matters that his fellow humanists failed to acknowledge. The next step in religion, he admitted, would require "unembittered endurance";[74] it would be no easy task, as some humanist thinkers seemed to imply. Moreover, Slaten (who called for the construction of a philosophy, not a religion—another point of divergence with some of his colleagues) refused to depend on evolution or a cosmic process for the construction of meaning. Unlike Reese and Dietrich, who sought to discover meaning in the cosmos and then cooperate with its processes, Slaten announced that the external gave no purpose, that "if human life is to have meaning, we must give it meaning by picking out a Goal of history, a discerned objective, and then struggling toward it."[75] These differences are subtle, to be sure, but not insignificant.

With the addition of Slaten and such others as Ernest Caldecott of Schnectady, Frank Wicks of Indianapolis, and Leon M. Birkhead of Kansas City to the humanist ranks, the movement began to take on a genuinely national scope, and by 1926, the new faith was in full swing. That also was the year Charles Francis Potter completed his conversion to the humanist point of view. Given the flamboyant influence Potter would exert over the next few years, it is worth saying a few words about him.

## Charles Francis Potter

The son of poor Baptist parents, Potter was licensed by the Baptist Church to preach at the age of seventeen. He slowly drifted away from that communion, however, under the influence of the works of the German theologian Adolf Harnack (which he absorbed while studying at Brown University) and the insights of higher criticism (with which he became acquainted during his years at Newton Theological Institute). In 1914, at the age of twenty-eight, Potter resigned from the Baptist Church and became a Unitarian, although his theological position at that time was hardly a developed one.

During Potter's first Unitarian pastorate, in Edmonton, Alberta, Canada (1914–1916), he was informed by a member of his congregation that the Unitarian minister in Spokane, Washington, a man named Dietrich, was "another maverick like you." "Neither of you," continued Potter's informant, "is really what is commonly called a Unitarian or even a Christian. He calls himself a Humanist; you say you're a Personalist. But as far as I can determine, you both are preaching the same line of thought."[76] Just a short time later, Lewis G. Wilson, then secretary of the AUA, similarly suggested to Potter that he had a good deal in common with one Curtis Reese of Des Moines.[77] Even though Potter entered into correspondence with these two eminent figures at this time, he was not yet ready to subscribe publicly to humanism himself.

Potter's successful ministry at the West Side Unitarian Church in New York City (1919–1925) was highlighted by the national attention he received from two events. The first was a famous series of debates in 1923–1924 with Dr. John Roach Stratton, minister of Calvary Baptist Church in New York and leader of the fundamentalist cause in the eastern United States. While only four of the originally scheduled five debates were ever held[78] and the victories were evenly split, Potter was widely acclaimed for his intellectual command and argumentative skills. His Baptist training had stood him in good stead, for he could draw upon many experiences and resources not readily available to the majority of liberal ministers.[79] The second event that brought attention to Potter's ministry was the Scopes trial, at which Potter assisted Clarence Darrow. Calling himself the "Bible expert for the defense," Potter worked up a list of inaccurate statements in the Holy Writ, and although Darrow was able to use only a few of these errors, Potter earned more national renown.

At the time of the Stratton debates, Potter described his theology as being "deistic with a small mixture of pantheism,"[80] but by 1925, he had begun to move rapidly in the direction of nontheism. Resigning from his West Side Church (because he thought education was replacing religion in importance throughout the modern world), Potter took a development job with Antioch College. It was during this period that he came wholeheartedly to a humanist position. An article he wrote entitled "Humanism—Theism," which appeared in the *Antioch Blaze* and was reprinted in the *Christian Register*, quoted liberally from Dietrich and lent credence to the belief that Potter was moving forthrightly into the humanist camp.[81]

After a brief and unhappy ministry at the conservative Universalist Church of the Divine Paternity in New York City[82] (1927–1929), Potter broke with Unitarianism to form his own First Humanist Society of New York. A prodigious author who possessed a flair for attracting the spotlight, he probably did more than anyone else to publicize the humanist cause beyond Unitarian circles. His books *Humanism: A New Religion* (1930) and *Humanizing Religion* (1933) were popular best-sellers (even though Potter wanted to be known for his intellectual contributions and once rebuked Edwin H. Wilson for referring to him as "merely a popularizer").[83]

## Other Significant Events

Potter's movement toward humanism was not the only significant event for the new faith during 1925–1930. The pages of the *Christian Register* rang once more with controversy over humanism when, in February 1926, Rev. Alfred R. Hussey, responding to the question "Are Unitarians Christians?" severely criticized A. Wakefield Slaten for having answered no. Slaten was a perfect example, asserted Hussey, "of how the utmost radical can . . . be at heart a bigot and a tyrant." Hussey concluded that Slaten was "not fitted to be our spokesman, for he has not been with us [Unitarians] long enough to fully comprehend our point of view." Moreover, Hussey declared that whether the humanists liked it or not, they, too, were Christians, for their avowed purpose was to redeem humanity. "If this is not essential Christianity," remarked Hussey, "I know not what to call it."[84]

The following issue of the *Christian Register* carried a similarly vitriolic attack upon the humanists by Rev. Maxwell Savage, who insisted that if he did not believe in God or immortality, he would certainly not call himself a Unitarian and would feel that his ministerial mission was finished. Savage went on to ridicule the humanists' notion of immortality through influence and concluded with a renewed plea for something of a creed to define *Unitarian*.[85]

These two articles represented the harshest attacks on religious humanism in several years, and it is symptomatic of the degree to which humanism had been accepted within conventional Unitarian circles that they provoked only a limited number of replies. Even Dietrich's February 18, 1926, article "Humanism" (the first definitive statement on the topic by Dietrich in the *Register* since his short essay in 1919), which was published independent of the Hussey and Savage pieces and not intended to be a response to them, elicited barely a single letter to the editor.[86]

Three letters in reply to the theistic criticisms do bear noting, however, for they clarify certain issues. The first was Dietrich's counterplea to Hussey, in which the Minneapolis minister acknowledged that "Dr.

Slaten is guilty of the fatal error into which I once slipped of daring to speak for the Unitarians."[87] Dietrich went on to say, however, that since Christianity had no monopoly on good works, there was no good reason to identify humanism (which rejected the central tenet of Christianity, namely, that Jesus was in some way different from all other humans) with Christianity. Instead, Dietrich suggested, perhaps all religions should identify with the inclusive term *humanism*, since a commitment to humanity's welfare was what they all presumably had in common.[88]

The second letter of interest was from Reese and constituted a "plea for discrimination" between humanism and other thought systems. He insisted that humanism is not materialism (which is mechanistic, while humanism is organic); not positivism (which worships humanity, while humanism holds that "Humanity is an abstraction having no concrete counterpart in objective reality"); not rationalism (which worships reason dogmatically, while humanism depends on intelligence and experience and trusts even them only experimentally); and not atheism (which is a denial of God, while humanism takes a position of inquiry).[89] Reese's letter remains one of the most compact statements ever penned differentiating humanism from other philosophies. Furthermore, it reinforces the contention that religious humanism saw itself distinct not only from Christian modernism, on its immediate right, but also from the radical parties of doubt, on its immediate left.

The third letter, contributed by Rev. Augustus Reccord, suggested that humanism was merely an early, undeveloped stage of theism and that if theists like himself would only be patient, humanists would overcome their immanentalist limitations and move into a greater glory. Humanism, said Reccord, is "simply a rational theism," and quoting Scripture, he condescendingly urged theists to bear with their humanist friends, "lest we bring down . . . the rebuke of the Almighty: 'All these years have I borne with them. Can ye not bear with them for a few days?'"[90] Reccord's letter is typical of a second stage of response that some theists had entered, and it is a prelude to a note he offered in the July 28, 1927, *Register* to which the new generation of humanists at Meadville Theological School replied.

William James once cited three classic stages in the life of a theory. First, any new theory "is attacked as absurd; then it is admitted to be true, but obvious and insignificant; finally, it is seen to be so important that its adversaries claim that they themselves discovered it."[91] By 1926, not all theists were attacking humanism in the manner of Hussey and Savage or in the tradition of Dodson and Sullivan. Some, like Reccord, had moved into the second and third stages of James's description.

Humanism was far from absurd; it was an important, if incomplete, insight. In fact, it was so important that theism encompassed it completely as, in the popular phraseology, "humanism plus!" Theism not only contained and even celebrated the values and commitments of humanism; it went further.

Dr. Charles E. Park, a distinguished theist from Boston, articulated this point of view in 1929: Humanism, he said, is a noble protest against the anthropomorphic and Calvinistic interpretations of God; likewise, it is a valuable check against the hypocritical misuse of the term *God*. But the humanist's vision of God (and Park will not allow that a humanist can be an atheist) is too limited. According to Park,

> The theist says that we are part of God's being; God is both in us and around us. The humanist says that God is part of our being; the divine in man is God. Theism declares that God is more than his creation; he is inexhaustible. Humanism claims that God is exhausted in his creation; his being is coterminous with man. . . . Your humanist . . . confines himself to as much of God as he can reasonably apprehend. . . . Theism is "humanism plus." The theist goes on speculating and adoring beyond the limits of human experience.[92]

Theism as "humanism plus" was a frequent cry among theistic advocates throughout the last half of the 1920s and into the 1930s, for it was a convenient way of appearing conciliatory while absorbing the new and troublesome position into the older and more comfortable one. Then, too, the early humanists who had failed to distinguish their doctrine of God clearly enough had to share some of the blame. But understandably, the "humanism plus" ploy was frustrating to many humanists, and when Reccord repeated the assumption[93] in 1927, a group of Meadville Theological School students felt compelled to refute the claim:

> Dr. Reccord, in common with many theists apparently assumes that humanism is simply a convenient synonym for the social stress in religion, and that the humanist . . . hesitates to press forward to the length to which the theist is prepared to go. . . .On the contrary, . . . it is the humanist who is willing to go to the full limits of religious thought. The humanist does not fear to take hold of the concepts embodied in theism and submit them to rigorous analysis in the light of . . . the sciences. . . . [H]e does not hesitate to criticize and examine the most cherished of religious beliefs.[94]

The theologs concluded that humanism was a "formulated philosophy of life" that stood independently and was not "included within the scope of the historical theological systems." These remarks are of interest not only for their content with regard to "humanism plus" but also because they reflect the thinking and coming of age of a second generation of humanists.

# Bursting the
# Unitarian Bounds

Born as it was within Unitarianism, religious humanism would not remain tied to that one religious community but would gradually attract individuals who had no formal Unitarian affiliation. Among the most important of these was A. Eustace Haydon, professor of comparative religions at the University of Chicago and scholar of national renown.

## A. Eustace Haydon and the Second Generation

Exactly one decade (1916–1926) after Revs. John Dietrich and Curtis W. Reese pronounced their humanism to their congregations, a generation of humanists was emerging that would see the movement into the 1930s and beyond. Concentrated in Chicago—and, more specifically, at Meadville Theological School—this second generation[1] came under the formative influence of a triumvirate of leaders: Reese, who, as a denominational official headquartered in Chicago, served as a ministerial model and introduced the students to applied humanism as it was practiced in Western Unitarian Conference (WUC) churches; Charles Lyttle, a Meadville professor of church history, who taught the "provenance of humanism from Greco-Roman ethical philosophy and the Christian Humanism of the Renaissance";[2] and, most profoundly, Haydon. In addition to Dietrich, Reese, Roy Wood Sellars, and John Dewey, Haydon played a significant role in shaping the movement and the Humanist Manifesto.

After attending McMasters University in Toronto, Haydon, like Reese and Charles Francis Potter, had trained for the Baptist ministry and served several Baptist pastorates before coming to the University of Chicago, where, in 1918, he received his doctorate and became a member of the faculty. Haydon's studies in comparative religions had provoked a move away from the faith of his youth into a broadly constructed humanism that was grounded in his assumptions about the universal nature of religious inclinations. Never a rigid sectarian, Haydon first taught a class in humanism at the Hyde Park Baptist Church and then did supply preaching to the Unitarian Church in Madison, Wisconsin. Upon his retirement from the University of Chicago in 1945, he became leader of the Chicago Ethical Culture Society.

Haydon's principal contribution to religious humanism was to provide the movement with an anthropological understanding of religion as a human phenomenon manifested in a variety of forms. Beneath all the variations in ritual and doctrine was a goal common to all religions: the quest for a satisfying life. In prescientific times, human control of the world and the future had been tenuous. Human projects were bound to fail, and with each failure came a heightened interest in a "compensatory, unseen world of wish and ideal," in which failure was transformed into victory. Gradually, attention shifted from the practical rewards that would come in this other world to the achievement of "eternal harmony in a super-personal absolute." But the overall goal was still the same: a satisfactory life. One of the drawbacks of this emphasis upon the next world, however, was that religion forfeited much of its influence over large segments of life in this one. Now modern, cultural humanity was presented with a new opportunity. For the first time, a practical tool was available for actualizing the ideal life: Science made ritual unnecessary. Religion needed to assert its partnership with science, to serve as a synthesizing agent of secular concerns, and to provide a wide-angled focus of ideals and a guiding ethic for science's creation of the satisfactory life.[3]

Haydon's perspective permitted humanists to justify a religion without a theology. When understood properly, he said, religion did not need to involve a relationship with the supernatural, the transcendent, or God. It is, at base, a quest for the good life. It always involves a threefold complex of the ideal (of the good life), a program (for reaching it), and a cosmic setting or world view within which the first two are understood. The ideal *may* relate to a concept of God, as *may* the program, and the cosmic setting *may* be theological in nature. But they do not *have* to be—and that, for the humanists, was the important point. Haydon thought that theology had corrupted religion by identifying it with a particular set of beliefs. By seeing the universalities among various religions, one could see that religion was really about people seeking real values that may change from age to age. As Haydon put it, "[T]he ideal may be purely material and practical at one time, change to an other-worldly quest for eternal happiness in which the gods are very important because of human helplessness, and then return once more to the earth and a confidence in human powers and intelligence."[4] But in all cases, they were legitimate examples of religion.

Because Haydon had such a generous understanding of the universal religious quest, he was eager to repudiate the modernists' attempts to disown humanism as a form of religion—something he felt he had accomplished with his basic theory. Beyond that, his quarrel with modernism was with its timidity and backwardness: "Too much time has been wasted in an effort to make appear logical pre-scientific ideas that . . . never were logical. There are more important problems than the untangling of philosophical enigmas."[5] "The task of modernism," Haydon said,

> is not to find new truths attuned to life and thought in a new age but to reveal how in religion the old remains ever true though all else may change. . . . [Modernists practice] an orthodoxy eroded by the tides of science and the winds of social change. They are too sensitive to . . . science and . . . social maladjustment to be real fundamentalists but too fundamentalist to venture into the uncharted sea of religious humanism.[6]

Yet if the modernists were too cautious about science, Haydon could be too reckless in his accolades: "Through science man will become master of the earth and rise to undreamed heights. Science . . . will release the potentialities of every soul. . . . In the new world the production of sick souls will no longer be possible. . . . Purpose will be given to life. The old tragedies, the ancient evils will pass away."[7]

Whatever his faults, Haydon shaped the thinking of the new generation of religious humanists and molded the movement to his own point of view. Beyond his intellectual contributions, he was instrumental in encouraging the second generation in its most far-reaching and important project: the publishing of a magazine. When, in April 1928, the first issue of the *New Humanist* appeared, in mimeograph form, it did so with Haydon's support and blessing. After all, he was the one who had urged the formation of the magazine's founding organization, the Humanist Fellowship, in November 1927. A joint venture of students, professors, and recent graduates from Meadville and the University of Chicago Divinity School, the Fellowship sought to encourage humanist thought within the university and church communities and, eventually, thanks to the success of its magazine, throughout the intellectual world. Nothing could have been more appropriate than the Fellowship's voting Haydon its first honorary member in May 1928.

The formation of the Humanist Fellowship represented an attempt by the second generation to forge a vehicle for the expression of their own thought and to spread humanist work beyond the confines of the Unitarian Church to academic and other religious circles. Some in the new generation developed intellectual and philosophical commitments of their own, which were subtly distinct from the early Dietrich-Reese formulations. Although these emphases were not different or wide-spread enough to cause serious division among humanists (and most did not receive enough support to be reflected significantly in the Humanist Manifesto), they did point in several noteworthy directions: toward the development of new religious language and ritual, an acknowledgment of intuition and mystery, and a greater appreciation for tragedy.

In his criticism of modernism, Haydon suggested that old religious language be replaced with franker and more scientifically sophisticated prose. The burden of Haydon's contribution to humanism was, in fact, exactly his contention that humanism could discard the trappings of theological constructs and language and still retain its religious character.

With the very first issue of the *New Humanist*, its editors recognized that humanism needed to develop a liturgy of its own, and to that end they included a column entitled "The Humanist Pulpit" in every issue until January 1930.[8] Originally edited by A. Wakefield Slaten (and later by Edwin H. Wilson), this column served as a clearinghouse and resource for the sharing of humanist materials (for example, opening words, hymn lyrics, responsive readings, and the like). Said Slaten, "Humanists must dare to be creative. A new symbolism is needed, new wordings for . . . ceremonies, . . . new materials for use in memorial services (let us cease to call them 'funerals')."[9]

Edwin H. Wilson, then Unitarian minister in Dayton, Ohio, made the call explicit in an address to the WUC in May 1932. Characterizing the redefined use of theistic and traditional religious language as "pouring new wine into old skins," Wilson said that no liberal or humanist should be forced to "say with his lips what he does not believe in his heart." He went on to argue,

> That today we should be giving up service elements which have been hallowed by long usage and sanctified for the ritualist by their perfection of form, is accordingly not surprising. . . . The words that are dangerous are exactly those words which, having had their content evaporated from them by frequent and uncritical usage, have become vain repetitions and empty platitudes.[10]

In contrast to the hesitancy of Dietrich (and even more, Reese) to give up the word *God* and its attendant vocabulary, the new generation was willing to experiment with a new terminology in a conscious effort to develop uniquely humanist forms. On this first point, the Humanist Manifesto, even though it said little about worship or ritual, respected the bias of the younger humanists and would not contain references to traditional linguistic constructions.

A second contribution of the new generation was the greater value it placed on intuition and mystery. The early humanism of the founders (as well as that of Haydon) so stressed the objective, linear, scientific, and rational that some members of the second generation felt called upon to redress the balance. Science may be the authority for analytic knowledge, but religious qualities and feelings encourage an experience of the wholeness of being. Religion should appreciate the experiential dimension, not simply the cognitive. It was compelled to recognize, in addition to the utterly rational, what Raymond Bragg, a leader of the second generation, called "the sudden perception of unforeseen relationships" or "intuition." The new generation encouraged a kind of poetic naturalism to supplement the more linear writings of the older humanists. Dietrich, Reese, Potter, and Haydon had to think their way through their native Christianity into the new religion. But the younger humanists—more of whom were birthright Unitarians or had been introduced to the denomination at an early age—had their humanism presented to them fully made. Perhaps they could better afford to explore a variety of religious paths than their elders could.

One of the most articulate of these adventurers was Rev. Lester Mondale, who, writing in the *New Humanist*, urged that humanism "rise from the armchair" and confront the inner lives of flesh-and-blood human beings. Science may be the gospel of humanity's salvation, but "it also, by clearly limiting knowledge to higher authenticated theory and demonstration, makes the unknown wider than it ever before was dreamed to be." Rationalism is fine, said Mondale, except that it may never end:

> And Humanism . . . has ended . . . in the . . . predicament [of] endless defining and redefining, and . . . persisting discussion of its relation to the philosophies of New Realism, Deweyan Instrumentalism, and the ghosts of haunting positivisms and naturalisms. . . . Humanism . . . must also recognize the infinitude of mystery. The human being meets the mystery every day; he will not disregard it as some Humanists and Modernists would have him do.[11]

Mondale had been urged into the ministry by Dietrich and had gone to Harvard Divinity School as an orthodox humanist. While there, he became acquainted with personality theory and wrote a thesis on the lives of great religious figures. Doing so convinced him that Dietrich's position was insufficient in that it failed to recognize the importance of psychological needs in questing, religious persons.[12]

Mondale's views were a helpful corrective to the earlier narrowness of the movement but were not widely accepted by his colleagues, who, as the Manifesto said, recognized "no uniquely religious emotions and attitudes" but found their "religious emotions expressed in a heightened sense of personal life and in a cooperative effort to promote social well-being." There was little room for awe or mystery. Religious experience could not be differentiated from secular. Mondale's criticisms highlight a problematic aspect of the humanist position.

The third new theme among some in the younger generation was that of tragedy. Both Dietrich and Haydon occasionally expressed a sense of pain at the loss of the certainties that came to them from orthodoxy. But only one humanist—and he of the younger generation—ever dwelt upon that and other more troubling affairs at any great length. Most humanists tended to turn a sunny face to the world and ignore or stoically endure hardship or perhaps consign it to "those things remediable by science." But James H. Hart addressed tragedy directly in two brilliant essays in the *New Humanist*. In "The Lost Individual," he bemoaned the disappearance of a heritage of certitude and acknowledged his feelings of vulnerability before the universe:

> There is . . . no sense of an order over-arching and inter-penetrating our world. Nothing divine remains . . . in heaven or on earth. . . . The Divine has collapsed when we need it most, and left us at the mercy

of events. . . . The crazy chaos of experience, in which justice seems nothing much, and luck and fortune all powerful, is left as our portion. There is nothing beyond or behind the chaos on which we ground ourselves. The psalmist cried, . . . 'I will left mine eyes unto the hills.' . . . Lucky psalmist! . . . For all such mountains have for us been thrown into the valleys, and made one with the disorder round about.[13]

And in "A Religious Mood," Hart sketched a poignant confrontation with the knowledge that all things end:

There is no good life that is not tumbled into oblivion. . . . The reality, when experienced, wrings unceasing protest from the human heart. Yet . . . it remains . . . the darkest and most difficult experience man endures. The sufferer walks alone in the harsh, bitter land; and there is no help for him in the thought of science. . . . [It] cannot enter this region, much less bring it under control. . . . No doubt man has won many victories of which he may well sing with pride, but such pride seems vain and empty when love meets death and yet cannot die.[14]

After so much of the sweet good-heartedness of the conventional humanist, these simple words from Hart, straining toward an expression of unameliorated pain, are strangely refreshing. This was a dimension that the larger movement left virtually untouched, for as the Manifesto said, "We will learn to face the crises of life in terms of their . . . naturalness and probability. Reasonable and manly attitudes will be fostered. . . . [H]umanism will . . . discourage sentimental and unreal hopes and wishful thinking."

Even though Hart exerted some influence on Wilson and Bragg, he was a loner, a dedicated individualist who went his own way and unfortunately had little effect upon the movement as a whole. He refused to sign the Humanist Manifesto, finding its creedlike overtones distasteful. But he came the closest of any of the humanists to expressing what decades later would be described as "the existential mood."

## The New Humanist

If the second generation achieved only limited success in their first goal, which was to influence mainline humanist thought, they were significantly more effective in their institutional aim to broaden the constituency and appeal of humanism. The primary instrument of this accomplishment was the *New Humanist* magazine.[15] H. G. Creel was the first editor of the magazine and president of the Humanist Fellowship (of which, according to Creel, "about one-half . . . are also members of the Unitarian Church, . . . some are members of other churches, and some of no church").[16] Creel articulated one of the magazine's most important goals as follows: "Humanists have felt for a good while the need of a means of communication with each other and a medium for the exchange of humanistic ideas and reports of progress and projects."[17] And with the *New Humanist*, they finally had it.

A modest typewritten bulletin at its inception, this small magazine would evolve into the widely respected magazine the *Humanist* and be instrumental in the founding of the American Humanist Association. Initially written almost exclusively by the small coterie of its founders, it quickly attracted well-known academic authors, and by November 1930, when it first appeared in printed form, people of the stature of Henry Nelson Wieman, Walter Horton, Edwin E. Aubrey, and eventually John Dewey had become frequent contributors.

Creel gave up editorship of the magazine in the fall of 1929 in order to teach at Lombard College in Galesburg, Illinois (the Universalist college of which Reese was president), and his position was assumed by Harold Buschman, who then saw the magazine through its next five years, including the May–June 1933 edition, which marked the appearance of the Humanist Manifesto.

One of Buschman's major contributions to the journal was to shift its emphasis from that of a humanist house organ to a more diversified academic publication. That shift did not occur without some conflict. In the spring of 1931, for instance, Potter objected to the *New Humanist*'s not taking a strenuously prohumanist line, instead allowing theists and critics of humanism to publish in it as well. Potter intimated that he might be forced to start his own highly partisan journal.[18] This prompted a reply from the scholarly Buschman, who was never an ardent sectarian humanist and even refused to sign the Manifesto on the grounds that it excluded people—himself included—rather than open up the movement to them.[19] Buschman remarked to Potter, "I am reminded of Professor Haydon's remark that 'Humanism is a climate' and with that vagueness I am certainly in sympathy. We could very easily 'whoop it up' for humanism. . . . We are certain, however, that the wisdom of the world is not concentrated altogether in American Humanism."[20] Throughout its years, the *New Humanist* remained a magazine of high intellectual standards.

In the fall of 1935, Buschman moved from Chicago to take a position on the faculty of the University of Missouri at Kansas City. He relinquished the editorship to Bragg, who would soon succeed Dietrich as minister of the First Unitarian Society of Minneapolis. With the departure of Buschman, the publishing rights were transferred from Buschman and Wilson to a new organization, the Humanist Press Association (HPA), which was modeled after the British Rationalist Press Association. With Reese as president, Haydon as vice-president, and Wilson as secretary-treasurer (while continuing as managing editor of the magazine), the HPA continued publication of the *New Humanist* until its demise in the fall of 1936.

As humanism moved into the lean years of the mid 1930s, it became more difficult to maintain adequate financial support for the magazine (whose subscribers never numbered over one thousand). When the Third Unitarian Church of Chicago, of which Wilson was then minister, succumbed to fire in 1936, it became impossible for the managing editor to devote the necessary time to fund-raising for the journal. Four editions of the *New Humanist* were published in 1936, with the final one issued in the fall. Fortunately, the HPA continued to function, and in February 1938, it issued the first copy of an interim publication, the *Humanist Bulletin*, under Wilson' s editorship. In February 1941, the HPA voted to change its name to the American Humanist Association, and in the spring of that year, the first issue of the *Humanist* magazine appeared.[21]

In retrospect, it is remarkable that such an unpretentious journal, begun under such inauspicious circumstances, should have the wide-ranging impact that the *New Humanist* did. Perhaps more than anything else, it spread the humanist word to the universities and the larger American intellectual community.[22]

## New Institutions, New Voices

Two other topics should be touched upon in regard to the burgeoning of the young faith: the founding of a number of independent humanist societies and the unprecedented publication of books sympathetic to the humanist cause.

As noted earlier, Potter had quickly acquired a reputation for flamboyance and independence, and that prevented him from ever being fully accepted as a leader by the Unitarian or Chicago humanist establishments. Biographer Mason Olds describes him as possessing a "rebellious temperament,"[23] and a reading of his autobiography, *The Preacher and I* (1951), reveals a prodigious ego as well. Spurred on by his unhappy experience as minister of the Church of the Divine Paternity (Universalist) in New York City from 1927–1929, Potter was moved in 1929 to found the first independent humanist church. He had grown tired of what he considered the conservatism of even the Unitarian Church and was ever aware of the publicity that would be generated by establishment of a so-called humanist church. And so Potter set in motion his plan to fulfill what he called "the development of a seeking mind."[24] Describing the decision, he said,

> [A]fter my experience at Divine Paternity, where a trustee's wife with more discernment than most said to me: "You should hire a hall to preach your beliefs. They're probably true, and I personally like them, but your sermons simply are not at home under these Gothic arches"—I knew that an independent Humanist society was the answer.[25]

The first service of the new Humanist Society was held September 29, 1929, in Steinway Hall in New York City. Some two-hundred fifty people heard Potter preach on "A New Faith for a New Age," and hundreds more were turned away at the door. More than one hundred persons signed charter membership cards, and two weeks later, the Society was formally organized. The first humanist wedding service was conducted on November 2, 1929, and the first funeral on March 3, 1931.[26] For some twenty years, Potter's Society attracted regular notoriety as well as distinguished patrons until it finally succumbed to the exigencies of the postwar years.

While Potter was founding his Humanist Society in New York City, Rev. Theodore C. Abell was forming a similar organization on the West Coast. Abell had become minister of the Unitarian Society of Hollywood, California, on December 19, 1921, when the church claimed only eleven members. Through persistent work, including a joint radio broadcast in cooperation with the First Unitarian Society of Los Angeles, he was able to build membership to over 250. Given this dramatic growth, the Society moved into the Hollywood Playhouse in 1926. In 1928, Abell published the first edition of his own humanist magazine, a small-time house organ sheet whose slogan was "Not anti-God, but pro-Man." The following year, he led the Society out of the American Unitarian Association and founded the Hollywood Humanist Society, a venture carried on utterly independent of the Potter move in New York. Never one to cooperate extensively with his humanist peers, Abell ran a one-man operation, and for that reason, he was never asked to sign the Humanist Manifesto or to take part in the larger humanist movement.[27]

Two other independent groups of humanists banded together, both in 1933: one in Berkeley, California, and the other in Sioux City, Iowa. Rev. Eldred C. Vanderlaan—like Dietrich, an ex-Reformed minister— had assumed the ministry of the First Unitarian Church of Berkeley in 1926 but resigned in 1933 to take leadership of the Free Fellowship (Humanist), a position he held for two years until he returned to high school teaching.[28] Vanderlaan was a signer of the Manifesto. The other humanist group was founded by Rev. Gordon Kent, who was something of an outcast among his colleagues for his sensationalistic techniques, one of which included dimming the sanctuary lights during his medita- tion and easing them back on with the closing "Amen." Kent was an out- spoken soul, and at one WUC meeting, he proclaimed that his most religious experience had been sticking a knife into a cow's throat and watching the blood gush out. After that account, he was known to his colleagues as "Bucket of Blood" Kent.[29]

None of the four societies survived past the early 1950s, and one or two folded in a matter of years. Considering that they were all founded in the midst of the Great Depression, it is startling that they did as well as they did. In any case, they brought the humanist word to even more outside the Unitarian fold. Active cooperation among the groups was rare, however, and they played little part in the larger humanist story.

If humanism could be spread by radical sectarianism, it could also reach potential adherents more profitably through the wide circulation of books by prominent authors. The late 1920s provided humanism with the canon of books it so badly needed to make its message under- stood in detail. Between 1926 and 1929, twelve major volumes were issued that either directly or implicitly endorsed a nontheistic point of view. The earliest, and one of the most important, as noted elsewhere, was Reese's *Humanism* (1926), which filled the vacuum for a short yet sophisticated account of the new faith. His *Humanist Sermons* (1927) supplemented the earlier book with a concrete set of statements of applied humanism from a broad spectrum of views.

Max Otto's *Natural Laws and Human Hopes* (1926) started where his magnum opus, *Things and Ideals* (1924), had concluded. *Things and Ideals* sounded a call for philosophy to retreat from its preoccupation with abstractions and ultimates and to deal with human matters and values. It went on to sketch the old thoughts and habits that must be given up and urged a new, naturalistic perspective for confronting existence, establishing ideals, and realizing them. *Natural Laws and Human Hopes* sought to outline the ways science might be turned to human advantage. These two books, plus contacts with Haydon through the Unitarian church in Madison, Wisconsin, put Otto in touch with the larger movement and made him a revered figure to all.

In 1928, one of the most influential humanist books was published: Sellars's *Religion Coming of Age*. Sellars's earlier book, *The Next Step in Religion* (1916), had helped form the religious opinion of humanist pioneers, especially Dietrich. Sellars's later book similarly informed the second generation and made his highly technical philosophical work available in popular form, particularly as it addressed religious questions.

Three books by authors outside the immediate humanist fold also had great impact on the movement: Julian Huxley's *Religion without Revelation* (1928), Walter Lippmann's *Preface to Morals* (1929), and Joseph Wood Krutch's *The Modern Temper* (1929). Among the three, Huxley's work was favored because it retained religion via the conception of a "sense of sacredness" while managing to be hardheaded as well.[30] When asked why he was willing to discard the term *God* but not *religion*, Huxley explained that he refused to use *God* not on principal but as a matter of policy. "I am frightened," he said, "that the semi-liberal theologians of the future would half accept the impersonal God for themselves, but then pander to their intellectually weaker brethren by using it in the personal sense in public."[31] Humanists were proud to have Huxley aligned squarely in their camp. As previously noted, the Lippmann and Krutch books were hardly materials of mainline humanist thought, but they had their impact both constructively and by denoting an extreme to which most humanists were unwilling to go.

This spurt of publishing was capped in 1929 by a succession of books that enunciated a humanist perspective: Haydon's *Quest of the Ages*, John Randall's *Religion and the Modern World*, Harry Elmer Barnes's *Twilight of Christianity*, Edwin A. Burtt's *Religion in an Age of Science*, and, of course, Dewey's *Quest for Certainty*. By the end of 1929, the United States had been thrust into the Great Depression. Not only were the resources of the book-publishing world diminished, but the market for tracts that promoted a wholly naturalistic perspective also may have decreased in the midst of the disaster. Only a few more seminal humanist volumes were issued in this period: Potter's *Humanism: A*

*New Religion* (1930) and *Humanizing Religion* (1933), Reese's *Humanist Religion* (1931), and J. A. C. F. Auer's *Humanism States Its Case* (1933).

Even so, by the early 1930s, humanism had earned a respectable place in religious thought, thanks largely to the publication of these materials. It had a journal, an informal organization, a collection of publications, and a band of devotees, and it had withstood the onslaughts of theism and futilitarianism. The one thing it still lacked was a convenient writ. With the onset of the Great Depression, such a statement of faith appeared even more necessary.

# Making the Manifesto

Leon Birkhead was a showman. He began his career as a preacher in 1904 at the age of nineteen, serving the back-country Illinois circuit[1] and was ordained to the Methodist ministry in 1910. Birkhead quickly discovered, however, that midwestern Methodism was not yet ripe for a minister who held beauty contests on the church lawn;[2] so in 1915, he applied for and received Unitarian fellowship.

Birkhead's Unitarian ministries—two years in Wichita, Kansas, and twenty-two years in Kansas City, Missouri—were characterized by even less placidity than his Methodist ministry. In the midst of unalleviated drought one year, Kansas City ministers announced that they were turning in desperation to the Lord. Birkhead appeared at their prayer meeting sporting an umbrella, an item his colleagues had forgotten. "I take it I am the only member of the clergy who has any faith," he told a reporter.[3] Author Sinclair Lewis, of *Elmer Gantry* (1927) fame, took inspiration for many of the details about his title character from conversations with Birkhead, who presumably advised him of the seamier side of "the cloth." "Gawd, the novel goes swell," Lewis wrote his publisher, Alfred Harcourt, from Kansas City in 1926. "I have a perfect corker to assist me on it—the Rev. Dr. Birkhead. . . . He is giving me exactly the dope I need. Twenty new scenes appear every hour."[4] Clearly, Birkhead was not one to endear himself to his colleagues.

Given his penchant for publicity, then, it seems appropriate that it was Birkhead who first suggested to Raymond Bragg, Curtis W. Reese's successor as secretary of the Western Unitarian Conference (WUC), that a summary statement of religious humanism was needed in order to introduce the new faith quickly and easily to the religious world. Charles Francis Potter had also been clamoring for such a declaration, and he suggested that if it were managed properly, it would bring humanism an immense amount of good copy, to say nothing of new sympathizers.[5] As secretary of the WUC, Bragg had much occasion to travel throughout the Midwest and gauge the needs of the people. He, too, felt the time was ripe for some kind of definitive statement of humanism. But why right then?

The year was 1933. The Great Depression had struck in November 1929. By 1933, the United States was headed into its fourth straight year of economic distress. Franklin Roosevelt had been elected president, but the New Deal recovery programs would not take full effect for months.

The 1920s had been hectic years. The nation had been polarized by the raillery and radicalism of the "lost generation," which provided a counterpoint to the reactionism of Wall Street. Religion had appeared to lose its vibrancy, taking on a veneer of comfortable respectability. This decade had seen the birth of nontheistic humanism and antitheistic futilitarianism. In 1929, when humanist publishing reached its zenith, the stock market crashed, and with the coming of the Great Depression, the nation's attention turned to practical issues of survival.

The skeptical metaphysical speculations of the humanists and futilitarians hardly provided the kind of cosmic assurance an economically insecure people needed in a religion, nor did Christian liberalism seem able to meet those needs. Frederick Lewis Allen described the move away from doubt and back into the safety of the traditional religious fold. With the depression, he observed, the theme of futility played itself out: "[T]he voice of science no longer seemed to deny so loudly and authoritatively the existence of spiritual values in the universe. . . . [F]ewer young men and women bustled with hostility toward any and all religion and there was a more widespread desire, even among the doubters, to find some ground for a positive and fruitful approach to life."[6]

At the same time, economic upheaval had generated genuine doubts about capitalism. What would have been labeled Red-inspired political and economic theories in the early 1920s had gained a semblance of respectability by the end of the decade. What everyone lacked in 1933 was confidence; what they sought was security—in orthodox religion and in experimental economics. "The only thing we have to fear is fear itself," said Roosevelt, and he sought to supply that confidence by instituting new and bold economic programs. While the new president could handle the technical problems, liberal religionists sought to reevaluate the contribution they might make in the arena of theological debate.

Two articles—both by humanists—that appeared in January 1933 issues of the *Christian Register* provide clues to the humanist response. The first, entitled "Dare Liberals Lead?" was by Ernest Caldecott, minister of the Unitarian Church in Schenectady, New York, and soon to be a signer of the Humanist Manifesto. In this article, Caldecott asserted that technical solutions to the economic dilemma required a solid philosophical foundation, and he challenged liberalism to come up with one:

> Any planned economy must take account of the facts of human nature. Liberals, not being extremists, recognize both the frailties and the possibilities of man. The ethicist and the economist must join forces for the good of the race. Assuming the technician . . . will take adequate care of the mechanics of subsistence, dare the liberal lead in ethics? . . . A cloister philosophy . . . will not meet modern needs. . . . The market for experimentation must be the new order. No longer can we endure the disparity between ideal and action.[7]

Two weeks later, Reese articulated four liberal philosophical principles that he insisted must underlie any satisfactory economic planning. New economic experimentation, he said, had to maximize personal liberty, recognize the primacy of personal rights before property rights, assert that science makes possible intelligent control of nature for human ends, and consistently heed the interdependency of all people and their needs and goals.[8]

Liberalism did not have to be divested of religious influence in the face of economic distress. With the promise of Roosevelt's political and economic liberalism in the wind and the increased acceptability of radical thought, humanism might be encouraged to enunciate its values in a public and forthright way—and to do so with some expectation of providing an appealing alternative to religious orthodoxy.

Thus, the Humanist Manifesto should be seen as both a theological and a political document. That its authors fully recognized the social urgencies of the day is attested to by the Manifesto's opening sentences ("Science and economic change have disrupted the old beliefs. Religions . . . [must come] to terms with new conditions created by vastly increased knowledge and experience.") and by the inclusion of the fourteenth point, which decried the profit-motivated society as inadequate and called for radical economic change.[9] The bulk of the document is philosophical, however, and may be seen to have dual purposes: to respond to the decline in popular appeal of humanistic and futilitarian doubt caused by the terror of the Depression and, at the same time, to take advantage of society's greater openness toward dissenting opinion and the renewed hopes that Roosevelt's election brought. Charles Lyttle said of the Manifesto, "It sought to replace despondency and doubt of God's loving Providence by confidence in the power of human intelligence and co-operative good will to become its own Providence."[10] The Manifesto was thus humanism's rallying call to overcome social anguish by solely human means. It was an attempt to reinstate the self-confidence and faith that Roosevelt's famous comment about fear had identified as missing.

On a less macrocosmic level, the Manifesto sought to consolidate the advances that humanism had made in the 1920s but that were threatened with eclipse by the Depression. Religious humanism was also confounded by the proliferation of other kinds of humanism—in particular, literary humanism. Said Allen, "[V]ery few who diligently talked about it [humanism] were clear as to which of three or four varieties of humanism they had in mind."[11] In part, the Manifesto was designed to clarify for the public just what kind of belief religious humanism represented. Only three years before, the movement had acquired a printed journal of its own. By 1933, publication of religious humanist texts had tapered off, but enthusiasm for strengthening the humanist hold still seemed strong, particularly in the universities. The creation of the Humanist Manifesto can be seen both as climaxing a period of growth that was in danger of ending and as reflecting the hope that the document might serve as a medium of consolidation for an independent humanist movement far into the future. This is the context in which Birkhead and Bragg operated. Quite understandably, they felt the need of the hour was publicity. Bragg set out in quest of it.

## The Initial Efforts

Perhaps more than any other thinker, Roy Wood Sellars had articulated humanism in a systematic and intellectually sophisticated way. While the work of Dietrich and Reese was seminal, they were clergy first, not professional philosophers. Haydon's scholarly attention was concentrated in one particular approach to religious issues and lacked Sellars's scope and depth. And Dewey, though hugely influential, was only peripherally associated with the organized movement.

Sellars was both a widely heralded philosopher and an ardent humanist. His technical works—*Critical Realism* (1916), *Evolutionary*

*Naturalism* (1922), *The Principles and Problems of Philosophy* (1926), and *The Philosophy of Physical Realism* (1932)—had gained him prominence among his peers while his more popular publications on religion— *The Next Step in Religion* (1918) and *Religion Coming of Age* (1928)—had shaped humanist thought for a decade and a half. These last two books successfully integrated Sellars's refined philosophy with the practical questions of religion and provided a well-constructed foundation upon which to build a systematic religious humanism.

It was fitting, therefore, that Bragg—who, as WUC secretary, had met Sellars a few years earlier on a trip to Ann Arbor[12]—should turn to him for the construction of a definitive statement of humanism. Sellars could be counted upon to combine intellect with a devotion to the welfare of the humanist cause.

In the early fall of 1932, Bragg seized upon an opportunity to propose his project. Headquartered as he was in Chicago (at the offices of the WUC on South Dearborn Street, the same address that served as the publication offices for the *New Humanist*), Bragg had many opportunities to attend lectures by renowned scholars at his alma mater, the University of Chicago, and he discovered to his delight one day that Professor Sellars was to speak on ethics. Immediately following the lecture, Bragg approached his friend and suggested that the philosopher draft a statement of humanist consensus. Smitten with the idea, Sellars asked that Bragg write him details and, upon receiving the secretary's letter, readily agreed to the assignment. Within six to eight weeks (around the turn of the year), the original draft of what Sellars dubbed "A Humanist Manifesto" was in Bragg's hands.[13]

Pleased to have such an academically reputable working document, Bragg called together three other prominent Chicago humanists— Haydon, Reese (then director of the Abraham Lincoln Center), and Wilson (minister of Third Unitarian Church on the city's west side)—to review the Sellars draft.[14] Unfortunately, that original draft has been lost. Historians can only speculate, therefore, as to the extent of the revisions that this four-member review committee instituted. "The frame of the Manifesto as finally published is essentially what it was when received in the first draft,"[15] Bragg recalled, but the contents were changed considerably. Meeting on at least three separate occasions (always in Reese's study at the Abraham Lincoln Center), the Chicago committee debated each point of the Manifesto with care, considering substantive issues as well as matters of expression. "When we agreed we had done with it what we wanted done, it was sent back to Sellars," Bragg wrote later. "I recall his response almost as if it were yesterday: 'You fellows have done a good job.'"[16]

The committee members had not done that job by themselves, however. At least five other persons were consulted in these initial stages: A. C. Fagginer Auer at Harvard; E. Burdette Backus, then recently resigned minister of the First Unitarian Church of Los Angeles; Leon M. Birkhead of Kansas City, the original proposer of the document; Albert C. Dieffenbach, recently resigned editor of the *Christian Register*, who had begun a term as religion editor of the Boston *Evening Transcript* and who ministered to the Unitarian Church in Newton Centre, Massachusetts; and John Dietrich.[17] Upon reviewing the working draft, these individuals' opinions were solicited and their suggestions evaluated. Auer, for example, described his involvement with the earliest versions of the Manifesto: "[A] copy was sent to me immediately after it had been drawn up and it was a carefully written statement. Indeed, in many points it did not resemble the present Manifesto. I recollect that Albert Dieffenbach and I worked some four or five hours over it in order to eliminate a number of inaccuracies, both historical and metaphysical."[18]

Despite these contributions, Bragg, Haydon, Reese, and Wilson took primary responsibility during the first three months of 1933 to work the Manifesto into presentable form. Of these four, Haydon's influence was clearly preeminent. He was, after all, the only academic scholar of the group and was revered by Bragg and Wilson (and, to a lesser extent, Reese) as a beloved mentor and teacher. The three introductory paragraphs largely reflect Haydon's thought and were likely the most prominent addition to Sellars's original attempt. (There is no way of knowing for sure, however, given the absence of that initial draft.) What is clear is that the committee, having consulted with the select group with whom the initial draft had been shared and having received Sellars's blessing of the earliest revisions, set about the task of introducing the Manifesto to a larger audience.

A target date for release was established: The Humanist Manifesto would be ready for distribution on May 1, 1933. This date was chosen, in part, by accident. Bragg had plans to be in the East in late April, and the committee decided that the most effective way to publicize the Manifesto would be for Bragg to confer at that time with the religion editor of the Associated Press in New York, indicate to him the nature of the document, and hope that the Associated Press would pick up the story.[19] The May 1 date would also allow the Manifesto to be carried prominently in the May–June issue of the *New Humanist*. But the target date caused something of a rush, for it was not until around April 1 that Bragg sent out copies of the first public draft with a request that signatures be returned by April 10. That meant the committee had less than a month to gather signatures, make the corrections and changes, and get the final draft back to all the signers for one last confirmation. For Bragg and Wilson, the month of April was consumed with the business of making the Manifesto.

Around April 1, Bragg issued the first public draft of the Manifesto (the only draft which is extant, other than the final) to a select group of thirty or more and accompanied the document with an explanatory letter on *New Humanist* stationery. (Wilson also signed a few of these cover letters.) This letter, marked "confidential," acknowledged that the purpose of the Manifesto was to secure press coverage for humanism and "to clarify the public mind" as to the movement's tenets. "The Manifesto," Bragg explained, "has been through many drafts and revisions [by Sellars, the committee, and its initial consultants] and represents a synthesis rather than the views of one person." Only a limited number of the many appropriate persons could be asked to sign, the letter went on, and "selection has been made upon the basis of published views of the man, upon the fields of work in which they [sic] are active, and upon geographical location." Finally, Bragg urged, "In order that this statement may be fully effective and constitute news when the signing is completed, we ask you kindly to keep the project a matter of strictest confidence until the release has appeared in the newspaper." He closed with a call for reactions and signatures and signed the letter "For the committee."[20]

One of the most intriguing questions is how it was determined who would receive this first public draft—that is, who would be asked to sign. The process, it appears, was highly informal; the members of the Chicago committee simply decided among themselves who should be approached. The major criteria seem to have been first, personal acquaintance, and second, intellectual contribution to humanist studies. Many whose support was solicited had published material in the *New Humanist*; several others were widely known public figures whose basic philosophical position appeared to be humanistic and/or who were personal heroes to members of the committee. In light of the concern to gain publicity for the release, there was, naturally, interest in attaching the names of well-known persons to the Manifesto. In addition to the prominent figures who did return their signatures, a number of others were probably asked but either refused or never responded to the inquiry, including Clarence Darrow, Harry Overstreet, Walter Lippmann, Paul Blanchard, Rabbi Maurice Eisendrath, and Professors Charles Beard, Hartley Grattan, J. Harvey Robinson, Lewis Mumford, C. J. Keyser, T. V. Smith, and Arthur Morgan.

## Edwin A. Burtt's Suggestions

Of all the respondents to Bragg's early April circulation of the first public draft, the one whose suggestions for changes had the most influence was Edwin A. Burtt of the Sage School of Philosophy at Cornell University. Burtt had become acquainted with religious humanism while on the faculty of the University of Chicago (1923–1932) and, in 1929, had published *Religion in the Age of Science* as part of a series edited by the famous naturalistic philosopher, John Herman Randall Jr., of Columbia, Missouri, another signer of the Manifesto. Although Burtt had moved to Ithaca in 1932 to teach at Cornell, he was still highly regarded by members of the Chicago committee. When they received a letter from him, dated April 10, 1933, begging that the Manifesto be withheld until he had had time to make some critical suggestions,[21] they were more than willing to comply. Burtt wrote, "I am sure that a manifesto in this form will distress and alienate from the humanist movement a large number of people whom it is not at all necessary to alienate," and he cited three objections: (1) The statement seemed to endorse a limited kind of naturalism; (2) it denied the reality of all entities transcending human experience, whereas Burtt understood humanism to require only that such entities be interpreted in terms "derived solely from human experience"; and (3) it denied the legitimacy of carrying over traditional religious terminology, whereas Burtt thought such terminology need only be reinterpreted "consistent with scientific truth and shareable human values."[22]

Before he had even received a reply to his letter, Burtt wrote again, making his suggestions concrete. In addition to a number of minor changes, many of which were adopted, he made five substantive proposals, three of which were essentially accepted.

Burtt's first successful revision was of the fifth point of the Manifesto, which in the original public draft had read, "The nature of the universe as depicted by modern science makes unacceptable any supernatural or cosmic guarantees of human values. Religion must formulate its hopes and plans in the light of scientific procedure." Of this paragraph, the Cornell philosopher said,

> Between the fifth and sixth theses, as they stand, it would seem to me very important to assert another, reading in substance as follows: "In denying the supernatural humanism does not deny the existence of realities transcending human experience. But it insists that the only dependable way of determining the meaning and value for us of such realities, as of any others, is by the honest study and intelligent assessment of human experiences of value realized in relation to such realities.[23]

In striking a compromise, the Chicago committee refused to leave the way quite so open as Burtt would have it for "realities transcending . . . experience." But they did add the following sentence, which stands in the fifth point between the two sentences of the original public draft: "Obviously humanism does not deny the possibility of realities as yet undiscovered, but it does insist that the way to determine the existence and value of any and all realities is by means of intelligent inquiry and by the assessment of their relation to human needs."

Burtt also was successful in modifying the thirteenth point of the Manifesto, which initially read, "Religious humanism maintains that all associations and institutions exist for the fulfillment of human life. The intelligent evaluation, transformation, control, and direction of such associations and institutions with a view of the enhancement of human life is the purpose and program of humanism." Burtt made this suggestion:

> Since it is absurd to expect the organization of the church, the ministry, etc., to remain the same when the accompanying theology has been exploded, I should insert between the thirteenth and fourteenth theses another reading: "Humanism expects that religious associations will pass through a progressive remolding, as experience teaches the best methods by which humanists may cooperatively further their common aims."[24]

The committee looked with favor upon this proposal and added the following third sentence to the two sentences of the original: "Certainly religious institutions, their ritualistic forms, ecclesiastical methods, and communal activities must be reconstituted as rapidly as experience allows, in order to function effectively in the modern world."

Burtt's final successful addition was to the fourteenth point, which originally read,

> The humanists are firmly convinced that existing acquisitive and profit-motivated society has shown itself to be inadequate and that a radical change in methods, controls, and motives must be instituted. A socialized and cooperative economic order must be established to the end that the equitable distribution of the means of life be possible. Humanists demand a shared life in a shared world.

Of this, the philosopher remarked, "I also feel some sort of gap between the fourteenth and fifteenth theses which could be remedied by the insertion of a thesis like this: 'The ultimate goal of humanism is the universal cooperation of mankind in intelligent pursuit of the common good.'"[25] The committee agreed fully and inserted this sentence between the second and third sentences of the original fourteenth point: "The goal of humanism is a free and universal society in which people voluntarily and intelligently cooperate for the common good."

Burtt's success in implementing these changes indicates he had significant influence with the committee. Even so, he was not influential enough to carry every issue; indeed, two of his proposals were rejected, although neither upon the committee's authority alone. In the first place, Burtt had urged revision of the third point, which first read, "Mind is a function of the organism. The traditional dualism of spirit and body must be rejected." He had suggested that it should be altered to read, "Mind and body are closely interconnected. Mind for many seems reasonably interpreted as a function of the body, certainly."[26] He favored this alteration, explained Burtt, because "the third thesis, as it stands, might seem to claim conclusiveness on a matter which science has not yet conclusively decided and to commit humanism to the old-fashioned sort of materialism."[27]

Others had also been troubled by Sellars's sweeping rejection of mind-body dualism (although something on that order did seem critical to a humanistic posture), and so, to settle the case, Wilson wrote Randall for his opinion on this and other Burtt suggestions. When Randall replied, "I object to Burtt's change in the third thesis,"[28] the committee accepted his judgment and settled on this final form of the third point: "Holding an organic view of life, humanists find that the traditional dualism of mind and body must be rejected."

Burtt's other unsuccessful addition was to the sixth point, which said simply, "We assert that the time has passed for theism, deism, modernism, and the several varieties of 'new thought.'" He urged the committee to add the following guideline: "If terms such as God, salvation, soul and the like are to be retained in humanist thought at all, they must be reinterpreted without reservation in terms of verifiable scientific knowledge and empirically discoverable human values."[29] Here was the old modernist-humanist linguistic bugaboo, and Burtt's suggestion could hardly appeal to many humanists, who had taken pains to avoid what they considered a faulty or even dishonest form of expression. But the committee, still eager to receive broad-based support, recognized that Burtt's change in the sixth point met "the needs of men such as John Haynes Holmes and others who have been sympathetic but critical thus far"[30] (that is, the less radical thinkers who could, in Holmes's words, "see [no] necessary contradiction between humanism . . . and theism"[31]).

As a conciliatory gesture, the committee tentatively included Burtt's sentence in a copy of the Manifesto, which went to, among others, Robert Morse Lovett, professor of English at the University of Chicago and member of the editorial board of the *New Republic*. On April 20, Lovett replied,

> In article [point] six, I think it is rather absurd to instruct people as to how they shall use certain words. These words have a metaphorical value in literature and I should say it was impossible to use them to symbolize "veritable scientific knowledge," etc. . . . Personally, I cannot give up the word God in such expressions as "God damn it all," any more than I can give up liquor. I resent the must, in both cases.[32]

This was enough of an objection to sanction Bragg and the committee's reversing their previous "half-hearted" decision to include the Burtt sentence, and so it was finally struck, leaving the sixth point as a simple statement that "the time is past for theism." It is interesting that the loophole for modernism that Burtt attempted to provide was not rejected on religious or philosophical grounds (as Dietrich or Sellars might have had it) but on semantic grounds. Lovett's argument, cogent though it may have been, hardly reflected most humanists' objections to so-called God-language.

In light of the interpretation that Burtt was to put upon humanism six years later in his *Types of Religious Philosophy* (1939)—namely, that it was simply an outgrowth of modernism and Christian liberalism—his suggested revisions (particularly of the fifth and sixth points) are hardly surprising. Furthermore, Burtt had always sought to reconcile divergent philosophical positions. He was concerned not to exclude from intellectual fellowship those who held humanistic beliefs that they expressed in nonhumanistic terminology. Of this basic posture, he wrote,

> [E]very sincerely championed philosophy has some constructive insight that ought not to be lost. . . . [T]he promising path ahead became for me the path of responsive openness to every . . . insight and of a zest to see how the partial truths thus glimpsed might be brought together in a coherent, all-embracing perspective. . . . My special talent lay largely in suggesting ways in which elements that most thinkers seem content to leave separated might be brought together in a constructive unity.[33]

Burtt's criticisms were taken so seriously by the committee because he was highly respected and many of his comments seemed to make sense. His exorbitant influence upon the remaking of the Manifesto may also be accounted for by the fact that he was the only professionally trained philosopher who responded to the April mailing with detailed suggestions of revisions. Others, including Max Otto and F. C. S. Schiller, responded negatively, and still others, such as Randall and Dewey, responded only perfunctorily. That Burtt was the catalyst of so many changes was therefore somewhat accidental. Finally, as noted previously, the changes Burtt initiated were designed to attract a broader spectrum of signers. When it became obvious that Holmes and those of his stripe would not sign, there was less reason, pressure, or need for the committee to retain some of the compromise language. The overriding fact about the Manifesto, which must always be kept in mind, is the collaborative, consensus-seeking nature of its construction.

## The Signers

The final alterations of the Humanist Manifesto were completed and the final version was mailed out around May 1.[34] Thirty-four persons were listed in the May–June 1933 issue of the *New Humanist* as signatories. (A thirty-fifth, Rev. Alson Robinson, returned his signature too late for publication.) The Manifesto was accompanied by an article by Sellars asserting that humanism goes beyond even the fundamentals of modernism (that is, "a belief in a regnant God, the validity of prayer and worship, and the acceptance of personal immortality") and making clear that this "religion adjusted to an intelligent naturalism" was very definitely not theistic:

> Upon this I think all naturalists are agreed that between naturalism and theism it is a case of either-or. Either a reality corresponding to the God-idea is at the center of reality in a directing, planning way or there is no such reality. In the latter case man is left to work out his own salvation as best he can with a fairly stable planet beneath his feet. His is the adventure and the goal.[35]

It is little wonder that the more theologically oriented humanists (such as Holmes, Burtt, and David Rhys Williams) felt some discomfort with the Manifesto's declarations—and they were not alone. A number of others who consented to have their names attached to the Manifesto did so with reservations about specific clauses. Randall, for instance, wrote the committee, "I very much dislike the crass optimism of the last two sentences,"[36] a prophetic criticism that would come back to haunt humanism with the political developments of the next two decades.[37] Lester Mondale questioned the rigidly naturalistic metaphysics of the document,[38] and David Rhys Williams took exception to the third point's identification of mind and body.

But many other signers either praised the statement or returned their signatures without comment. The most prominent of the latter was Professor John Dewey. Bragg had written him on April 13, soliciting his criticisms of the first public draft,[39] but Dewey simply returned the draft without comment and added his signature. In light of the criticism Dewey received upon signing the Manifesto and given the excessive pride the humanists took in adding his name to the list, it is fascinating to note that he had absolutely no direct influence upon the writing of the declaration. Even though the promoters of the Manifesto often represented Dewey's lack of critical response as a wholehearted endorsement of their work, it may instead be only an indication that the great philosopher was too busy to study or comment upon the document.

Perhaps the most striking feature of the group of signers is their high educational attainment. All but three (Floyd, Jones, and Shipley) of the thirty-four signers held degrees beyond the undergraduate, and thirteen held the doctorate of philosophy or equivalent. This was, without exception, an intellectually competent group. The religion they would promote was bound to be commensurate with those intellectual virtues. It did not have to be complex, but it surely would not be simple.

Reasonably enough, given their educational levels, all but four (Floyd, Jones, Shipley, and Walker[40]) were either clergy or teachers, and of the latter, the best-represented discipline was philosophy (with five). Thus, it seems safe to conclude that, beyond being a somewhat sophisticated faith, religious humanism was unlikely to be philosophically vacuous. (Its presuppositions and conclusions might be considered wrong, but at least there were good reasons for persons to affirm those doctrines.) With an overabundance of ministers and professors, however, there was perhaps a tendency to the abstract and a failure to speak in terms readily available to the average citizen.

Although all the signers were well educated, they do fall into two groups: the scholars, who provided the foundation for the faith, and the popularizers (the ministers plus Floyd et al.), who appropriated those convictions and made them available to the humanist public. Some evidence points to occasional tension between the two, but for the most part, each respected the domain and expertise of the other. In fact, some of the clergy (for example, Reese and Mondale) contributed to the movement's intellectual development, and some of the professors (including Auer and Haydon) participated in the ecclesiastical.

It is also interesting to look at the negative responses of some who, though generally sympathetic to humanism, could not bring themselves to be associated with the Humanist Manifesto. Many of the well-known individuals who were approached—such as Walter Lippmann, Clarence Darrow, Lewis Mumford, and Paul Blanchard—simply failed to reply at all. But a score or so sent explanations of their disaffection, and four of the most important of these were carried in the May–June issue of the *New Humanist* alongside the Manifesto.

The problems that Buschman (still editor of the *New Humanist*) and Otto had with the document were formal, rather than substantive. "Any creed excludes and this is no exception," said Buschman, who was, at this time, associated with the Ethical Culture Movement.[41] And Otto, always a rigorous individualist who required that action be linked to rhetoric, claimed, "Humanism cannot be 'sold' to people. . . . And experience has taught me to beware of deceiving myself into thinking something has really been done when . . . something has been said."[42]

The two other demurring essays in the *New Humanist* struck at the content of the document in a more complex fashion. Holmes, taking his familiar modernist position, objected strenuously to the sixth point: "Theism is to my mind the blossom which grows upon the plant of humanism. . . . God is only another word for humanity." He went on to say of the spirit of the sixth point, "You are arbitrarily ruling out from our thought something about which you know absolutely nothing at all."[43] Finally, Arthur E. Morgan contributed a long and rambling essay that eschewed humanism's lack of faith, ridiculed its cocksureness, and objected to its refusal to entertain "wishful thinking."[44]

Several academic figures whose books had touched upon humanist concerns and influenced the movement never responded to invitations to sign or comment upon the Manifesto. They included Hartley Grattan, author of *The Critique of Humanism* (1930), a response to Irving Babbitt's literary humanism, and J. Harvey Robinson, whose *The Mind in the Making* (1921) and *The Humanizing of Knowledge* (1924) had argued for the synthesizing of knowledge in pursuit of social ends and in general had promoted precise, scientific thought. But one well-known thinker, F. C. S. Schiller, with whose work the humanists had long identified, sent a caustic note of disdain:

> I have expressed my opinion about your sort of "Humanism" in the article I have contributed to the *Encyclopedia of The Social Sciences*, vol. VII, and there is, I think, nothing in your Manifesto which requires me to modify it. I note that your Manifesto has 15 articles, 50 percent more than the Ten Commandments and one more even than President Wilson's Fourteen Points. Its general attitude is that of what was formerly . . . described as Positivism. . . . So the propriety of the name Humanism is not apparent to me. Regarded as a religious program, it seems to me to suffer from vagueness and weakness on its constructive side, and it seems difficult to understand why anyone holding its views should wish to associate himself in an organization. . . . But undoubtedly man is a very social and sociable animal.[45]

No doubt, at least part of Schiller's contempt derived from the fact that he had appropriated the term *humanism* to describe his own idiosyncratic philosophy and did not care to have competitors.[46]

The desire of the editors of the Humanist Manifesto to receive the endorsement of practicing scientists for their new religion prompted invitations to physiologist A. J. Carlson, medical doctor Bernard Fantus, and popular science lecturer Maynard Shipley—all of whom signed. But renowned astronomer Harlow Shapley, who had served for thirty-one years as director of the Harvard College Observatory, was less cooperative. While Shapley subscribed to the principles of the movement "almost in toto," he wrote, "I wonder if we are ready for a religion of intelligence; and if so, is it spontaneous enough, when nurtured by a deliberate manifesto?" Furthermore, the astronomer begged to be exempted from making judgments in the religious field: "I feel that my sphere of activity should remain in the . . . interpretation of stars . . . and expanding universes—relatively simple enterprises—and that I should not venture . . . into the complicated neuroses that we call civilization." Shapley did not sign the Manifesto, but he did bring one insightful criticism to bear upon it, asking, "Is the word religion correctly used?" referring to the seventh point's definition of religion as including everything "humanly significant." "Your affirmation," he went on, "defines it so broadly that I suggest the word *life* or *activity* as equally appropriate."[47]

How ironic that a scientist was the one to raise such an appropriate question, particularly in light of his professed ignorance of religious matters. The editors of the Manifesto could hardly give much credence to Shapley's criticism, of course, eager as they were to follow Haydon's lead in asserting that religion was, at heart, a quest for the satisfying life, rather than a preoccupation with some differentiated realm. If these early humanists had been willing to call their system a philosophy, rather than a religion, they would have been able to avoid this pitfall.

Few social scientists were invited to sign the humanist document, in part, because Watsonian behaviorism reigned during these years and thus little sympathy could be found in the fledgling social sciences for a humanistic posture. One of those who was asked to sign, University of Chicago economist Frank Knight, declined with an objection to the fourteenth point's call for a "socialized and cooperative economic order." And the one sociologist who did become a signatory, Frank H. Hankins of Smith College, similarly demurred:

> I think there is no doubt [he wrote Wilson] that the 14th point . . . is more or less ambiguous. . . . Personally, I would not wish to commit myself to . . . anything like a Socialist creed. My sociological theory is that every society makes some sort of amalgam of individualism, state socialism, and communism. This amalgam, moreover, changes with every fundamental change in the material basis of culture. It is therefore unscientific as well as unwise to commit oneself to *a prioristic* or

dogmatic statement of just what combination of these principles should be made at any time. Personally, I should hope that "a socialized and cooperative economic order" could be established without surrendering very important values in the principles of individual liberty, initiative and private property.[48]

It is interesting, given the controversial history of the fourteenth point, that the two professional social scientists among the list of invitees both expressed caution about it in the first place.

The failure to solicit a signature from the great philosopher Bertrand Russell is somewhat curious, particularly in light of the approaches made to Lippmann and Darrow. Russell might be classified with them as a futilitarian, but his views were certainly at least of secondary support to many humanists. Perhaps the committee was aware that Russell would have been less than receptive to an organized movement of their ilk. "I prefer to use the old term 'rationalism,'" he is purported to have written to Corliss Lamont,[49] and on another occasion, he was quoted as saying, "I should not have any inclination to call myself a humanist, as I think, on the whole, that the non-human part of the cosmos is much more interesting and satisfactory than the human part."[50] In any case, Russell was never contacted formally by the committee.[51]

In addition to famous persons and scientists, the organizers of the drive for signers wanted to elicit support from individuals of religious persuasions other than Unitarian. Fifteen of the thirty-four final signatories held Unitarian fellowship.[52] One of these, W. Frank Swift, was an Ethical Culture leader, a faith also subscribed to by one of the lay signers, V. T. Thayer, director of the Ethical Culture Schools in New York City. Rev. Clinton Lee Scott was a Universalist and Charles Francis Potter, a Humanist, but the only clergyperson of any other affiliation to sign the document was Rabbi Jacob J. Weinstein, then advisor to Jewish Students at Columbia University.

Several other rabbis were approached by the committee but rejected the invitation, feeling the need to avoid a diminution of Jewish solidarity. Rabbi Maurice Eisendrath of Toronto, for example, initially endorsed the *New Humanist*, saying, "There is today no more vital religious movement than that known as The New Humanism. . . . The *New Humanist* is filling a need long felt by religious liberals."[53] He rescinded his support, however, in the face of a perceived need for Jews to unite against anti-Semitism.[54] Similarly, Rabbi Joseph L. Baron of Milwaukee, while taking minimal exception to the substance of the Manifesto, observed,

> Your stress on metaphysical affirmations and denials may inject a theological polemic in liberal synagogues, where the membership is not concerned with the definition of God or of the hereafter but with practical problems such as the application of the ideals of justice and peace, the upbuilding of a Jewish civilization in Palestine, the combat against tyranny, fanaticism, etc. To divert the attention of the Jewish congregation, and to divide its forces, by declarations against "theism . . ." would be an unfortunate obstacle in the path of its humanistic leaders who are endeavoring to mobilize its strength toward the achievement of a "socialized and cooperative" way of life.[55]

Rabbi Weinstein apparently came to a like conclusion in short order and recanted his humanist associations. Six years after having signed the Manifesto, he became the rabbi of a major Jewish temple in Chicago and served there over thirty years. He retracted his support for humanism in this period of his career, which perhaps indicates that nonparish clergy can afford to take more radical stands than those who serve congregations.[56]

If the committee was concerned with achieving some kind of religious balance, it was far less cognizant of other demographic considerations, as were most white males of that day. No people of color were asked to sign and only one woman was: Mary McDowell, founder of the University of Chicago's Settlement House and an associate of Reese. McDowell did not sign the Manifesto, however, and her reason for declining is not in the record.

One final group of nonsigners that should not be overlooked were those Unitarian clergy like Holmes, who had, at one time or another, been sympathetically identified (sometimes only by rumor) with humanism but who, for various reasons, could not bring themselves to associate with the Manifesto. Perhaps the most prominent humanist minister among the defectors was Hart, who asked, "Must humanists swear by Haydon and Sellars?" He went on to say, "As for any social program—concrete and provoking—I don't find anything but mere words. . . . It appears to me that some of the 'academic' humanists are still verbalizing mainly."[57] Given Hart's personal orientation, which was so different from that of his fellow humanists, and his close friendship and respect for Max Otto, it is not surprising that he refused to join the other signers.

Other ministers who declined to sign were E. Stanton Hodgin of New Bedford, Massachusetts; Miles Hanson, Jr., of Weston, Massachusetts; W. Hanson Pulsford of Chicago; Walton E. Cole of Toledo; Bruce Swift of Buffalo; and Hugh Tigner of Oneonta, New York. Swift, convinced that the Manifesto was "unnecessarily hazy" and lacking in literary value,[58] rewrote the document completely in what he considered more flowing prose, but his "alternative Manifesto" was virtually ignored by the committee. Tigner was even harsher in his criticism, claiming (1) that the Manifesto lacked humility and that science could make no verifiable statements about the nature of the universe; (2) that humanism lacked a program and was little more than an "arm-chair" religion "seeing vision in its pipesmoke" ("I fail to see," wrote Tigner, "how humanism is more worthwhile than liberal Christianity—the last word in ineffectuality"); and (3) that humanism was an "academic" religion that "may please a few anemic professors" but is without social or spiritual substance.[59] However cogent his criticisms, Tigner was a fringe figure on the humanist scene, and his remarks were not taken seriously.

Undeterred by the criticism—that the Manifesto constituted a creed; that the time was not right; that the document was philosophically in error; that it would alienate the modernists; that it was a program without substance and rhetoric without results—the committee pushed on. The final task was to set the document before the larger public. And in that regard, the promoters met with only moderate success.

# Return to the Fold

As he had planned, Raymond Bragg had a conversation with the religion editor of the Associated Press (AP), and the Humanist Manifesto was released exclusively to that news service. While it hardly made front-page news, stories about the document were carried in several major newspapers. The New York *Herald Tribune* devoted half a column to the story, as did the Chicago *Evening Post* (one of whose former staff members, Llewelyn Jones, had signed the Manifesto). The *New York Times*, however, ignored the release completely. In most places, the story was relegated to the religion page.

## Publicity and Reaction

This indifference to the release of the Manifesto made it evident that neither Bragg nor Edwin H. Wilson possessed the public relations expertise to secure comprehensive national publicity. Charles Francis Potter complained to them about this in a letter dated May 1, 1933, immediately after the Manifesto's release. In the first place, Potter wrote harpingly, the story should have been given to all three wire services, for if one gets information before the others, the neglected two will boycott the release (which, in fact, they did). Second, Potter pointed out that advance copies of the Manifesto should have gone to independent columnists, and a press release heralding the coming event should have been circulated preceding the issue date of the *New Humanist*. Said Potter of the *Times*'s neglecting the story,

> If you had wired me, as I suggested, I could have seen the editor, whom I know personally and . . . impressed him with the significance of the thing and he would have got [sic] Dewey, Barnes, or Randall on the wire for a local supplementary statement. . . . The *Daily News* ran a little story. The *World Telegram* had nothing, but that was because UP [United Press] didn't have the release.[1]

No doubt, Potter's ire stemmed, in part, from the fact that his letter of signature-authorization had been accompanied by some suggestions about the public release of the Manifesto. He wrote,

> [T]he Manifesto is too long, too verbose and too academic for newspaper editors to handle. The fifteen points might well be boiled down to ten, for they overlap considerably. . . . [I]f it is sent out as it is to the leading newspapers, . . . it will get a two-stick write-up in a few of the papers. If it must go out as it is, it should be accompanied by an explanatory and summarizing release.[2]

Even though no one was as conscientious or as skilled as Potter in securing public notice, his suggestions were largely ignored. The Manifesto suffered the consequences in terms of lack of coverage.

Two major magazines did pick up the story from the AP release and published short references. *Time* carried a one-column article about the Manifesto in its religion section, giving a straightforward, if capsulized, recounting of its content. "Humanism," said *Time*, "used to be a good subject for parlor and dinner table discussions. Few people knew what it actually was or where literary humanism left off and religious humanism began."[3] *Time*'s comments reinforce the theory that the Manifesto's publication was a rear-guard action and that one of the motivations behind it was to distinguish religious humanism from its nominal counterparts.

In contrast to the *Time* report, the short article in the *Literary Digest* was loaded with sarcasm about the document "offered by the thirty-four [signers]—nearly three times the number of those first to spread the gospel." Before supplying the gist of the Manifesto, the *Digest* satirized it:

> Let the supernatural go; abandon the hope learned in Sunday School and at mother's knee. Let science rule the conscience. . . . So, in short, say these teachers of youth. . . . Easter Day was not far behind when this statement was issued and the tens of thousands who attended dawn services . . . may be sufficient to show that the creedless creed has not many converts yet.[4]

The *Digest* went on to list all the professors who had signed the document plus Rabbi Jacob J. Weinstein but none of the other clergy or laity, which is testimony to the weight lent the Manifesto by its prestigious academic supporters.

Reaction from the religious press was similarly disappointing. If the committee had expected the Manifesto to create a new humanist-theist tempest, they had miscalculated. Publication of the Manifesto in both the Unitarian *Christian Register* (May 11, 1933) and the Universalist *Christian Leader* (May 13, 1933) elicited a dearth of reactions. There was no resurgence of the acrimony that had scorched the *Register's* pages a decade and a half before. Leslie Pennington, writing in the Unitarian journal two weeks after the appearance of the Manifesto, criticized the sweeping rejection of theism but took a broadly sympathetic view.[5] Even the editor of the *Christian Leader*, John van Schaik, vigorously reasserted the place of "God omnipotent, omniscient, good, real, objective, personal, and super-personal . . . the God and Father of Our Lord Jesus Christ" yet acknowledged that humanism represented an important view "too often obscured and neglected."[6] Few letters to the editor followed these remarks.

The *Standard*, the journal of the Ethical Culture movement, supported the document in large part but raised an interesting objection:

> We do not as societies seek to make . . . regard for . . . better human relations, greater justice, truthfulness, sympathy, tolerance, disinterestedness . . . depend on any doctrine such as those [in the Manifesto.] . . . There must be room in our fellowship . . . for those to whom the garnered moral experience of mankind . . . demands supreme allegiance, whether the cosmos favors it or not, and whether there is a supersensible reality or not. . . . Every newly-labeled religion . . . is, alas, liable to be a new means of intellectualist separatism.[7]

Perhaps the most virulent response from a Christian journal was supplied in the June 7, 1933, issue of the *Christian Century*. In general, the *Century* agreed with the Manifesto's second, fourth, seventh, eighth, twelfth, thirteenth, fourteenth, and fifteenth points. But with regard to the first point, it claimed scientific support for the universe's being "both self-existent and created." It accepted the third point with qualifications, while it challenged outright the fifth, sixth, ninth, tenth, and eleventh points. The *Century* editorial summarized the magazine's objections this way:

> We affirm that the thing of which man is becoming aware is that he alone is not responsible for ["the world of his dreams."] . . . His man-made social order has broken down because he has taken no account of his cosmic Partner in this great business, and as he surveys the wreck of his efforts, he is just beginning to awaken to the fact that

there exists in the universe beyond his egoistic, humanistic self, a living Power, or Process, or Something (we will not now use the word "God"[8]) with which he must work in a spirit of self-subordination . . . if he is to realize the world of his dreams.[9]

Perhaps what outraged the *Century* more than anything else was that John Dewey had signed the humanist declaration when it "moves in a different realm from that which Mr. Dewey's own interpretation of nature and experience has opened up to the modern mind." As the leading modernist journal of the day, the *Century* was particularly concerned with defending a liberal Christian faith that was obviously under attack in the Manifesto, and a defection from the theist ranks of someone as prominent as Dewey could not help but be annoying and threatening. Interestingly enough (and in keeping with its modernist sophistication), the *Century* attacked the Manifesto on philosophical, not religious, grounds, saying, "The humanists may call this by the name 'religion' if they wish to, but they have no business to call it philosophy."[10] This ploy may have taken the humanists off guard, given how careful they had been to define religion so as to include themselves within its rubric. They could never have suspected they might be attacked as unphilosophical.

The critical temper of the *Century*'s article was contradicted by the remarks of other theists, who, as William James had predicted, were in the process of virtually claiming that they had discovered the more beneficent principles of humanism themselves. Far from deprecating the Manifesto entirely, James Luther Adams remarked that "some humanists are simply reacting against inadequate conceptions of God." Dr. Russell Henry Stafford, pastor of Old South Congregational Church in Boston, found much to sympathize with, and Dwight Bradley of the First Congregational Church in Newton, Massachusetts, declared, "I'd accept the Humanist Manifesto and its fifteen points without a cavil, but I should want to add a great deal more to it." Even a Catholic, Father Michael Ahern, "found himself in some agreement."[11] The days when humanism shocked the religious world in the United States were on the wane.

## Unitarianism and Humanism

Humanism represented a natural step in the evolution of left-wing Unitarianism out of the late-nineteenth-century Free Religion/Western Unitarian Conference controversies. But virtually all the signers of the Manifesto (Wilson is a prominent exception) and absolutely all the

founders of the new faith (namely, Dietrich, Reese, Slaten, and Potter)
had come to Unitarianism from other denominations.

Religious humanism, though invented and nurtured by Unitarian
clergy, was not initiated by persons whose roots were sunk deep in
Unitarian soil. None of the major humanists had even been raised in
churches affected by the free-religion issue. On the contrary, they had
been brought up in non-Unitarian Christian churches, ranging in outlook from the relative modernism of Dietrich's Reformed Church and
Bragg's Congregational to the fundamentalism of Reese's Southern Baptist. In one sense these early humanists were outsiders to the Unitarian
fold who were attempting to apply their imprint to an already existing
institution. This may account, at least in part, for the fury of the theists
during the early days of the controversy.

Religious humanism in its first decade must be interpreted as little
more than a phenomenon internal to Unitarianism. It was a type,
branch, or wing of Unitarianism at this point (although not one endemic
to Unitarianism). From a theist's point of view, it was more like a disease
that had invaded the body of the church at its weakest point: the
western extension.

By the time the Manifesto appeared, however, humanism had burst
its Unitarian bounds and was taking on an independence of sorts. While
retaining much of its Unitarian flavor (and affiliation), it was attracting
persons from other liberal religious backgrounds as well as persons without noticeable religious associations. The problem was that in the early
1930s, humanism had no independent organizational structure of its
own, thanks largely to the fact that it had been dependent for so long
upon Unitarianism for its institutional identity. Instead, humanism was a
loose conglomeration of individuals drawn largely from a narrow arena:
primarily, universities and left-wing churches. Only the Humanist Press
Association (HPA) might be considered a central institutional body, and
it was pitifully amorphous in its constitution. Not until 1941, with the
founding of the American Humanist Association, did secular humanism
have a formal organization of its own, significantly independent of
Unitarianism. What kind of religious body was religious humanism as it
struggled to assert a separate identity?

## The Sociology of Religious Humanism

Religious organizations have traditionally been characterized as either
churches or sects, depending upon their traits. Humanism obviously
did not constitute a church, but was it a sect? Ernst Troeltsch's famous

definition holds that a *sect* represents a radical revolt against the secularizing tendencies of the church. It is a call to return to true first principles and usually involves rejection of the secular world in favor of an ascetic loyalty and regimen. Commonly found among the lower class and frequently accounted for as a reaction to economic deprivation, its traits include

> lay Christianity, personal achievement in ethics and religion, the radical fellowship of love, . . . indifference toward the authority of the state and the ruling classes, . . . the separation of the religious life from the economic struggle by means of the ideal of poverty and frugality, . . . the directness of the personal religious relationship, criticism of official spiritual guides and theologians, the appeal to the New Testament and Primitive Church.[12]

In large part, these are clearly not the characteristics of religious humanism. Far from requiring a return to the church's primitive past, humanism sought the authority of a realm previously considered antithetical to true religion—that is, science. Far from demanding a retreat from the secular, humanism embraced it in the name of the religious. And far from being a movement of people who were economically disadvantaged, humanism was a religion of the upper middle class.

In broader terms, however, religious humanism does share some of the traditional characteristics of a sect: It emerged out of a segment of an established church; it was critical of established theologians; it called for the embrace of a tightly delineated set of doctrines; it was largely lay oriented outside of Unitarianism; and as a significant separate movement, it lasted but one generation and then found itself largely absorbed by the established church. It may not have been a sect, but in some respects, it was sect-like.

The most common characteristic of those who form radical religious groups (sects) has been understood to be a sense of alienation. In what ways might the signers of the Manifesto exhibit evidence of alienation from the world about them? A brief review of their biographies (see Appendix A) suggests that the most remarkably common feature among a majority of the thirty-four signers was that they had attained significantly higher educational and professional status than their parents had. Whereas most of the fathers of the signers had no college education and were employed in unskilled or semiskilled vocations,[13] their sons were all well educated and prestigiously employed. The signers, then, were part of an upwardly mobile generation, the first in their families to attain a high level of status. Several were even immigrants who had gone on to achieve highly respected positions in their new society.[14]

As they were moving up the educational and professional ladders, however, the signers were also encountering a society much at odds with their own values. As described in earlier sections, American society of the first three decades of the twentieth century—particularly during the 1920s, when humanism flourished—was engaged in either making war or enjoying opulence. Wealth and conformity were valued more than intelligence and integrity by the larger society. The signers of the Manifesto had achieved some status beyond that of their parents, yet they still felt somewhat isolated from the standard American social milieu in terms of their values. Moreover, most of the humanists had come at quite an early age to reject normative religion and its apologetic for secular society.

When considered in sum, these qualities comprise the condition of alienation. In his classic essay "On the Meaning of Alienation," Melvin Seeman wrote,

> The fourth type of alienation refers to isolation. This usage is most  common in descriptions of the intellectual role, where writers refer to detachment of the intellectual from popular culture standards. The alienated in the isolation sense are those who . . . assign low reward value to goals or beliefs that are typically highly valued in the given society.[15]

This describes the intellectual humanist.

Thus, religious humanists found themselves at odds with the larger society. They did not value wealth (preferring "a shared life in a shared world"); capitalism (calling for a "socialized and cooperative economic order"); traditional religion or its goals (declaring that "the time has passed for theism" and calling for new goals of "a heightened sense of personal life and . . . a cooperative effort to promote social well-being"); competition (cherishing the cooperative use of intelligence); militarism ("affirming life rather than denying it"); or conformity (encouraging individuals in their idiosyncratic quests for truth and satisfaction). As upwardly mobile, first-generation achievers, they had not yet been so absorbed by the social system as to accept its values unequivocally or without question. Their roots in poverty and low social status (and, in many cases, in rural life) still clung to them. They could go one of two ways: Either follow a typical *nouveau-riche* pattern of utter absorption into conventionality, or assume a posture of rebellion, rejection, and isolation.

Probably due, in large part, to their educational attainments and professional associations, the signers chose the latter route. Robert Merton has described this response in terms of social structure. If the word *religious* is substituted for *social* in the following quotation, his words are aptly characteristic of the signers. Rebellion, he says, "leads men outside the environing social structure to envisage and seek to bring into being a new, that is to say, greatly modified, social structure. It presupposes alienation from reigning goals and standards."[16]

One of the major problems with the traditional theory of sects is that it has assumed that sects are grounded in economic deprivation. But religious humanism was a movement of the well-educated, intellectual class. Charles Y. Glock has provided a helpful extension of classical sect theory that expands the notion of deprivation. In addition to economic, social, and organismic deprivation, he says, religious groups may arise out of feelings of ethical deprivation. This exists "when the individual comes to feel that the dominant values of the society [and its normative religion] no longer provide him with a meaningful way of organizing his life, and that it is necessary for him to find an alternative. The deprivation is . . . a philosophical one."[17]

With this observation, Glock has helped to explain religious humanism. A movement of this type would not encourage a return to fundamental religious traditions since it is these very traditions that have been labeled unsatisfactory. In addition, this kind of sect has no need to repudiate secular society; on the contrary, it will approach what the eminent sociologist of religion J. Milton Yinger has called an "aggressive sect" that seeks to "alter the world by direct action . . . [and] shades off toward political . . . movements."[18] So there may still be room for religious humanism within a revised theory of sectarianism.

Yet the question posed by Schiller remains unanswered: "Why would persons so disparaging of traditional religious culture and so enamored of the secular associate in an ostensibly religious organization at all?" Once again, the answer seems to lie in the fact that the early religious humanists were only one generation away from a more traditional mindset. A surprising number of the signers were either the sons of ministers or had, at one time, been headed for their own careers in ministry. (And, of course, eighteen of them were clergy.) Even though they had rejected orthodoxy, they never quite lost the "religion bug." This, after all, was the difference between the humanists and Gertrude Stein's "lost generation": The former, while sharing many of the latter's grievances against the established church and theology, remained interested in the religious enterprise and sought to broaden and reform it.

Secular agencies and movements, says Glock, may satisfy the ethically deprived person as well as the religious. But while they both provide means of overcoming deprivation, they differ in source. Secular responses, such as the existentialist movement and the beatniks, are grounded in a complete and radical break with all the values of a society, including, for example, the promise of scientific development. Religious responses are more narrowly confined to an alienation from the dominant religious or philosophical system.[19] The "lost generation" was willing to sacrifice everything; religious humanists were only willing to give up established religion and some elements of the economic system. Two variables had to come together in order for a religious humanist to appear: (1) a belief in the need for a more intellectual (or empirically sophisticated) religion and (2) a lack of cynicism about religion in general and a willingness to involve oneself in a religious movement. Finding these variables in a single individual was comparatively rare, and hence, the group of humanists was comparatively small.

Religious humanism, as revealed in the Manifesto, was an intellectually sophisticated religion that was bound to appeal only to a limited segment of the population—specifically, the well educated—even under the most auspicious of circumstances, for at least three reasons. First, the substance of the faith was intellectually demanding, and few people had the philosophical equipment or acquaintance to absorb it. In addition, humanism was a faith being promoted primarily by the intellectual class in a highly cerebral, nonemotive fashion and therefore stimulated the kind of anti-intellectualism inherent in American culture. As such, it was unable to capitalize upon the fact that, as Richard Hofstadter pointed out, "In America religious culture has been largely shaped by the evangelical spirit."[20] Finally, without a referent to the transcendent, the Humanist Manifesto offered little comfort in time of crisis and required instead a highly philosophical understanding of suffering. ("Man will learn to face the crises of life in terms of his knowledge of their naturalness and probability. Reasonable and manly attitudes will be fostered by education and supported by custom.") Such sentiments might have attracted more sympathy in an optimistic period of history but failed to garner wide support in the face of economic decline.

Glock has written meaningfully about the temporary nature of groups on this order, and his comments apply to humanism:

> Movements which originate in ethical deprivation have a great propensity . . . to be short-lived. This is not because ethical deprivation is not a persistent element in society; there are always likely to be some individuals who feel that the dominant value system provides an inadequate answer to this concern. However, resolutions which seem appropriate at one time are not likely to be so at another. In effect, ethical deprivation tends to be subject to fade. Consequently, organizational responses . . . tend to capture attention for the moment and be quickly replaced. . . . In general, ethical deprivation characterizes only a small minority of a population at a given time and movements which respond to such deprivation are likely—whether they survive or not—always to be minority movements.[21]

Yinger has suggested that something like this is exactly what happened to religious humanism. Born in the postwar years of the late teens of the twentieth century, it took about fifteen years to develop. But as it did so, social changes of all sorts were taking place, particularly economic. Humanism simply could not keep pace with them.[22] Because it was such a relatively homogeneous perspective, it failed to be a broad enough or amorphous enough umbrella beneath which to contain the variety of viewpoints necessary to the long-term maintenance of a religious group. Established churches, like major political parties, survive exactly because they house a wide continuum of views; religious humanism narrowed the possibilities sharply and also failed to alter its perspective successfully enough to meet the changing social conditions. The result was numerical demise as an independent movement.

Secular humanism made its stand in the guise of the American Humanist Association. But religious humanism was largely absorbed back into Unitarianism, where most of its adherents reside today. Having rejected the Dodson-Sullivan campaign to exclude humanism on creedal grounds, Unitarianism, flexible as it is, was in a position to offer relatively unqualified support for religious humanists. Most humanists had little reason to desert Unitarianism, and attempts at independence may have been largely for the sake of those non-Unitarians or, more likely, nonchurched individuals who might affiliate with a movement as long as it was separate from the Unitarian denomination. The fact is that

Unitarianism has practiced with regard to humanism what church historian Martin Marty has indicated Christian churches have traditionally done with regard to all doubt: That is, it extended its boundaries enough to absorb the new stirrings and make a secessionist move unnecessary or at least unsuccessful.

Finally, a few more practical reasons may be offered for the decline of religious humanism. In an article entitled "Five Factors Crucial to the Growth and Spread of a Modern Religious Movement," Gerlach and Hines list these five factors: "(1) reticulate organization, (2) fervent and convincing recruitment along pre-existing lines of significant social relationships, (3) a commitment act or experience, (4) a change-oriented and action-motivating ideology which offers (a) a simple master plan presented in symbolic and easily communicated terms, (b) a sense of sharing in the control and rewards of destiny, (c) a feeling of personal worth and power, [and] (5) the perception of real or imagined opposition."[23] Of these five factors, humanism could claim only 4c (and possibly 4b) and 5.

The inchoate nature of the religious humanist organization has already been discussed. Recruitment was largely an unsystematic contacting of individuals, and except where it took place within the context of a local Unitarian church, it was highly idiosyncratic. Humanism had nothing resembling a commitment act or welcoming into fellowship (except as subscribing to the *New Humanist* might be so considered).

The ideology of humanism, while surely "change-oriented and action-motivating," offered no "simple master plan presented in symbolic and easily communicated terms." In fact, religious humanism largely avoided symbolism, preferring to speak instead in straightforward, secular terms. And to reiterate, the substance of the faith was hardly "easily communicated."

Whether humanism encouraged a "sense of sharing in the control and rewards of destiny" is debatable. It certainly supported the use of human intelligence in problem solving and the conviction that human beings could have a hand in their own future. But given its naturalistic bias, one may wonder how much it encouraged the notion that anyone or anything could "control . . . destiny."

Suffice it to say that religious humanism simply lacked the resources and structure for continued growth. Coupled with the previously cited social and institutional conditions, it could hardly help but subside in number and influence in a very short time.

## Attempts to Revise the Manifesto

Between 1939 and 1941, several attempts were made to revise or rewrite the Manifesto. Once again, the catalyst was Potter, who, in 1939, circulated a letter encouraging such revision in the direction of greater simplicity and enthusiasm. And once again, fearing Potter's publicity-seeking influence, the HPA usurped the project. A committee of the original draftees (plus Potter, Burtt, and Auer) was appointed, questionnaires were mailed to the living signers, but no reworking of the Manifesto was forthcoming. Apparently, too many people found the original draft sufficient or urged that it remain intact as a historical document. A year or so after his initial inquiries, Potter wrote Wilson bitterly,

> [After I wrote to all those people] . . . the HPA . . . jumped in and took charge of the thing. I meekly agreed. What happened? A committee was appointed of which I was one. It never met as far as I could learn, although I tried to get them together. . . . It just fizzled out. . . . The HPA has adopted a sort of dog-in-the-manger attitude about humanism which is hindering growth of the movement. The Unitarian connections of humanism have long since been outgrown.[24]

In 1953, talk of redoing the Manifesto was renewed, and in fact, comments were solicited from the signers and their responses "twenty years after" were printed in the *Humanist*. Auer, Birkhead, Caldecott, Jones, Lovett, Reese, Reiser, and Scott urged that nothing substantial be altered. Many persons, however, repudiated the fourteenth point's call for socialism, and Barnes even worried that humanists might be considered security risks because of it.

On July 24, 1952, the staff of the *Humanist* issued this statement: "It [the fourteenth point] reflects the outlook of depression times. . . . [M]any Humanists have come to the conclusion that Humanism ought not to enter as far into controversial realms as did point fourteen nor take an official position as a movement with regard to any particular economic system."[25]

Several persons suggested that the sixth point's sweeping rejection of theism be omitted and that room be left in the fifth point for cosmic guarantees of values. Mondale continued his campaign for recognition of humanity's tragic character. Potter called the Manifesto "antique and sententious, . . . verbose and dogmatic: even shrill at times," and Williams found the language "prosaic and . . . uninspiring."[26] Thayer doubted that the world was any longer rushing toward humanism (if indeed it ever had), and Weinstein signaled his retreat from humanism by calling it a "young man's faith." Perhaps John Herman Randall's comments were most striking:

> First, there is lacking any expression of a tragic sense of life. "Joy in liv-ing" (point 12) is not the only attitude religion must foster. There is also such a thing as humility. The inevitabilities of frustration and of evil . . . must be seen in proper perspective, but they must be seen. There is no reason why supernaturalism should be allowed a monop-oly on the religious expression of the tragic sense. Humanism can do it more effectively because more sanely. . . .
>
> Secondly, there is insufficient recognition of the need of imagina-tion in religion. . . . [N]o religion that tries to get along without any imaginative embodiment of its basic attitudes and values is likely to attract many. Humanism should face seriously the very difficult prob-lem of creating more adequate . . . symbols. It should at least recognize the need even if it cannot yet satisfy it.[27]

All this is not to say that the Manifesto had no impact at all or that the debate between theist and humanist had utterly ended. Within months and even years following publication of the Manifesto, theist would take on humanist or vice versa in a variety of forums (although rarely with debate focused solely upon the 1933 document). In the *Christian Register*, three such exchanges took place in the latter half of 1933: one between Andrew Banning and Roy Wood Sellars,[28] one between Louis Harap and John Dewey,[29] and one between Joseph Haroutunian and Fagginer Auer.[30] Even as late as 1951, J. A. C. Fagginer Auer and Julian Hartt tangled over theism and humanism.[31] Regardless, the evidence seems to point to the conclusion that the Humanist Mani-festo did not ride the crest of the wave but rather appeared after the wave had spilled.

The major theistic critiques of humanism—Willard Sperry's *Signs of These Times* (1929), Walter Marshall Horton's *Theism and the Modern Mood* (1930), and William P. King's *Humanism: Another Battle Line* (1931)—had been published several years before the coming of the Manifesto. And no major book-length critique from a learned theist refuting humanism appeared until Charles Hartshorne's *Beyond Humanism* (1937), four years after the Manifesto's construction.

Within Unitarianism, the controversy subsided in 1936 with Frederick May Eliot's election as president of the American Unitarian Association (AUA). Religious humanism was now a fully accepted theological option within that denomination. But as a separate, stand-alone movement, it never grew very large. By the mid 1930s, for all practical purposes, religious humanism as an independent institution had been catapulted into effective decline.

# The Signers of the Humanist Manifesto

This appendix contains biographical sketches of the thirty-four signers of the Humanist Manifesto of 1933. Only supplementary information is provided for those individuals whose stories are described in detail in the body of the text, if they are mentioned at all; those referred to briefly or not at all in the text are described in more detail here, where such detail is available. The number in parentheses after each signer's name indicates his age at the time of the signing.

JOHANNES ABRAHAM CHRISTOFFEL FAGGINER AUER (50), a native of Middleburg, The Netherlands, was professor of philosophy and church history at Tufts University from 1926–1930 and, in 1930, was appointed Parkman Professor of Church History and Theology at Harvard. A 1906 graduate of Meadville, Auer served churches in Wheeling, West Virginia; Ithaca, New York; and Concord, New Hampshire. He received his doctorate of philosophy from Cornell before taking up teaching in 1926.[1] His 1932 Lowell Institute lectures, delivered in King's Chapel, Boston, served as the basis for his book *Humanism States Its Case* (1933), which is considered an important contribution to popular humanist literature. The book did not sell well, however, due to the hard economic times, and Auer never completed a contemplated history of humanism. He provided scholarly and historical input to the humanist movement over the years and contributed to the early editing of the original Roy Wood Sellars draft of the Humanist Manifesto.

EDWIN BURDETTE BACKUS (45), born and raised in Blanchard, Ohio, was the son of a Unitarian minister father and a Universalist minister mother. He was educated at the University of Michigan and Meadville

Theological School. Backus's humanism dated back at least to his Erie, Pennsylvania, ministry (1917–1920).[2] He served Unitarian churches in Los Angeles, California; Des Moines, Iowa; and Indianapolis, Indiana, before his retirement. At the time of the Manifesto's publication, however, Backus was not employed due to ill health.[3]

HARRY ELMER BARNES (44) was born in Auburn, New York. He received his undergraduate degree from Syracuse University and his doctorate of philosophy in history from Columbia (1918); his dissertation was on the history of prison reform. Always a prominent academician, Barnes taught at Syracuse University, Columbia University, Barnard College, Clark University, The New School for Social Research, Amherst College, Smith College, Temple University, the University of Colorado, Indiana University, and Washington State College. When he signed the Manifesto, however, he was employed by the editorial department of the Scripps-Howard newspapers, a position he held from 1929–1940. Barnes gained the attention of the humanists with his *Twilight of Christianity* (1929), a book that disparaged religion, in general, while it specifically heralded the teachings of John Dietrich. A renowned figure long active in the struggle for prison reform and treatment of juvenile delinquency, Barnes was never a part of the inner circle of religious humanism, in part, because he was too radically nontheistic for many. Nonetheless, his name lent considerable prestige to the 1933 declaration.

LEON MILTON BIRKHEAD (48) was the son of a Winfield, Missouri, farmer. Two years after signing the Manifesto (and four years before his resignation from the Kansas City church), he took a trip to Germany that would change the direction of his life. While there, an official of Julius Streicher's propaganda organization boasted to Birkhead about the American citizens who were assisting the Nazis. Birkhead returned to the United States and plunged into a systematic investigation of pro-fascists such as Henry Ford, Father Coughlin, Gerald L. K. Smith, and the America First Committee. In 1937, Birkhead formed the Friends of Democracy (FOD) to help combat the perceived menace. He directed the FOD for a decade, turning his still potent publicity-generating capacities to a political end.[4] (In addition, he was a frequent contributor to Haldeman-Julius's series of political tracts known popularly as the "little blue books.") Birkhead's flair for the spectacular prevented him from making a substantive impact upon the humanist movement. Like Charles Francis Potter, he was rather a popularizer of the first order.

RAYMOND BENNETT BRAGG (30), the son of a Congregational family from Worcester, Massachusetts, was instrumental in the creation and dissemination of the Humanist Manifesto. Even though his father, a loom fixer, had only completed high school, he was an inveterate reader and "something of an eighteenth century deist" who encouraged his son's intellectual exploration.

During the young Bragg's first two years of college, at Bates, in Lewiston, Maine, he came under the influence of a geology professor, a member of the local Universalist Church, who promoted evolutionary theory in contradiction of biblical accounts and, in general, opened his students' eyes to the primacy of scientific inquiry. Bragg was introduced to Unitarianism after his transfer to Brown University, where Walter Goodnough Everett, the idealist professor of philosophy and member of First Parish Church in Providence, made a great impact on him. The type of Unitarianism Bragg became acquainted with in Providence and on trips home to Worcester (where the humanists' foe, Maxwell Savage, held the pulpit) was, however, of a distinctly conservative stripe.

The Bates geology professor had mentioned Meadville Theological School to him, and although Bragg had intended to become a historian, his growing philosophical maturity prompted him to consider the ministry; thus, he chose Meadville over the more theistic Harvard. In 1926, a year after taking up residence in Meadville, Pennsylvania, Bragg moved with the school to Chicago, where he found those formative factors that swayed him decisively to humanism. Foremost among these were A. Eustace Haydon and Curtis W. Reese (the latter of whom Bragg would succeed, at an unusually young age, as secretary of the Western Unitarian Conference [WUC]). Shirley Jackson Case, who taught primitive Christianity at the University of Chicago Divinity School and was author of the seminal *Jesus, A Social Biography*, was also an important figure in the young man's intellectual growth. Upon his graduation from Meadville in 1928, Bragg took up the ministry of the Unitarian Church in Evanston, Illinois, where he remained for slightly more than two years before going to the WUC and, later, the Unitarian Church in Kansas City, Missouri.[5]

EDWIN ARTHUR BURTT (age unknown) was born of profoundly religious parents: his mother a woman of "deep moral and spiritual understanding" and his father a zealous New England Baptist minister who broke away early "from the half-heartedness and pussyfooting compromises of religion" and took up work as a missionary in South China.[6] After four years of living with his family in China, Burtt began to question some of his father's theology (for instance, his father's belief that drugs should not be used to cure illness because God is the healer of all disease). He returned at age seventeen to the United States. But it was not until Burtt's years at Yale as an undergraduate and even more explicitly at Union Theological Seminary (where he went to study for the ministry) that these doubts were articulated in any systematic fashion.

Moving further in the direction of liberal Protestantism, Burtt was ordained a Presbyterian minister and briefly served in the Methodist ministry, as well. (At Union, liberal theologians Eugene Lyman and A. C. McGiffert were important influences upon him.) Within a short time, however, he had been won exclusively to philosophy as a profession and, having secured a doctorate of philosophy, took up teaching at Columbia in 1921. (He withdrew from the Presbyterian ministry in 1927.)

Burtt's early modernist idealism was modified by constant exposure to the philosophy of naturalism so prevalent at Columbia, which included Deweyan instrumentalism and neorealism. In 1923, the young philosopher moved to the University of Chicago, where he taught for the next nine years, and again, his naturalistic bias was reinforced by older colleagues, for whom that philosophy was primary. But even in his ardent humanist days, he refused to reject much that other humanists had discarded. Burtt's early religious exposure and his Eastern experience were beckoning him, and within ten years after signing the Manifesto, he retreated into a moderate position that, while it rejected supernaturalism, valued the mystery inherent in theism.

During World War II, Burtt cut his ties with humanism and joined the Society of Friends; his position at Cornell provided him the opportunity to teach courses in comparative religion, and he gradually incorporated much Eastern thought into his personal philosophical stance. But something of the humanist remained, for in a 1974 interview, he summarized his faith in these words: "The mystery of the divine is revealed no longer in nature but in the mystery which is man and his possibilities."[7] A gentle, introspective man, Burtt had never been a radical and is identified as one of the more conservative signers of the Manifesto.

ERNEST CALDECOTT (44) was born in Shropshire, England, the son of a flour and bread dealer. After graduating from Drew Theological School in 1916, he began his ministry in the Methodist Church. By 1919, he had moved beyond Methodism and taken up the Unitarian ministry in

Schenectady, New York, one of the earliest New York State churches to become humanist. His major settlement was at the First Unitarian Church of Los Angeles, where he succeeded E. Burdette Backus and remained for fourteen years,[8] always a champion of concrete action and liberal causes.[9] Although Caldecott was instrumental in applying humanism to issues in religious education, he was not a central figure in the movement.[10]

ANTON J. CARLSON (58), a University of Chicago scientist, was perhaps one of the most distinguished scholars to sign the Manifesto, along with Harry Elmer Barnes, John Dewey, and John Herman Randall, Jr. The son of a Swedish farmer, Carlson emigrated to the United States at the age of sixteen. Prevailed upon by a Swedish Lutheran minister to join his profession, Carlson began ten years of study at Augustana, a Swedish Lutheran institution in Minnesota. Even at this early age, his empirical nature began to emerge; the young theological student once proposed to a seminary class that they conduct a controlled experiment in the power of prayer. Despite his skepticism, Carlson took a church in Anaconda, Montana, which he served for one year, finally announcing to his startled congregation that what he had been preaching to them was nothing but a pack of lies.[11]

Renouncing the ministry, Carlson took up the study of physiology at the University of Chicago. He chose to become a scientist, not a philosopher, because the former profession allowed for empirical verification of its theories. He became a professor of physiology at Chicago in 1909 and chair of that department in 1916.

Always a rigorous empiricist, Carlson warred against scientific quackery. Once, in a debate with a Chicago mental telepathist, the "seer" told of how it had suddenly come to him at nine o'clock one evening that his mother in New York needed him desperately. Later, he said, he had learned that at exactly nine o'clock, his mother had fallen down the stairs and injured herself. "What do you think of that?" the telepathist challenged Carlson. "My first thought," replied the scientist, "is of the hour difference between Eastern and Central time."[12]

The recipient of many awards in his field, Carlson distinguished himself as president of the American Association for the Advancement of Sciences (AAAS) and the American Association of University Professors (AAUP). His commitments were not limited to the academic, however. Perhaps his finest hour came when he stood alone in opposition to the International Physiological Society holding a meeting in Rome because all Italian university professors had been forced to swear allegiance to Mussolini. In an address to the AAAS, Carlson posed the question: "Does the great understanding of man and nature increase the scientist's social responsibility?" His answer, a resounding yes, was matched by his deeds. Appropriately enough, Carlson was the first recipient of the Humanist of the Year award, presented to him by the American Humanist Association in 1953.

JOHN DEWEY (72), the great American educator and philosopher, was born in Burlington, Vermont. He graduated from the University of Vermont and received his doctorate of philosophy from Johns Hopkins in 1884. He taught at the universities of Minnesota (1888–1889), Michigan (1884–1888, 1889–1894), and Chicago (1894–1904) and at Columbia from 1904 until his retirement in 1930.

ALBERT C. DIEFFENBACH (56) was reared in the Reformed Church and studied for its ministry, serving his first church (the Reformed Church of the Ascension) in Pittsburgh, the same city where John Dietrich served his. In 1911, Dieffenbach resigned from the Reformed Church and entered into the Unitarian fellowship, taking as his first pulpit the Unitarian Church in Hartford, Connecticut. He stayed there five years until his appointment, in 1918, to the editorship of the *Christian Register*, a post he held until 1932.

By 1933, the former editor, now minister of a small New England church, felt comfortable enough to take part in both the drafting and the promotion of the Manifesto. That year, he also became religion editor of the *Boston Evening Transcript*, a position he retained until the paper suspended publication in 1941.

BERNARD FANTUS (age unknown) was the only medical doctor to sign the Manifesto. An authority on therapeutics, Fantus was a pioneer in the standardization of drugs, the originator of the blood bank in the United States and of so-called candy medication for children, the head of staff at the Illinois College of Medicine, the founder and director of the Department of Therapeutics at Cook County Hospital in Chicago, and, for many years, a member of Edwin H. Wilson's Third Unitarian Church in Chicago.

Fantus came to the United States from Vienna as a boy with his parents and younger brothers. His father, a printer, had harbored a desire to be a doctor and passed on his ambition to his oldest son. "David

Fantus would often tell his tiny son, 'You are going to be a doctor,' to which Bernard would confidently add: 'I'll be a professor too!'"[13] With a degree from the College of Physicians and Surgeons (paid for, at first, by his father's printing in lieu of tuition), his dream became a reality.

Fantus's humanism pervaded his professional practice, and he retained that faith until the day of his death. In fact, during his final illness, he composed his own "Humanist Affirmation," having long thought the Manifesto was too academic to reach many people.

WILLIAM FLOYD (62) was perhaps the most singular character among the signers of the Manifesto. Born into a wealthy old colonial family, Floyd was a descendent of Governor William Bradford of Plymouth Colony and great-great grandson of William Floyd, a signer of the Declaration of Independence. Educated at St. Marks School and Princeton University, the young Floyd became a Wall Street real estate broker, lord of a manorial estate on Long Island, and prominent member of New York City's Church of the Ascension (Episcopalian).

In the 1910s, this wealthy socialite experienced a radical transformation in both belief and life-style, attributed, in part, to his having read Thomas Paine's *The Age of Reason*. The upshot of this conversion was that Floyd gave up his Christianity to edit the *Arbitrator*, a humanist monthly he founded in 1918. In addition, he discarded his Republicanism in favor of pacifistic socialism and organized the Peace Patriots, a group dedicated to "Love of Country and Opposition to War."

In 1927, Floyd sold part of his Long Island estate (which had been in the family since the days of King James II) in order to finance the American Arbitration Crusade, an organization promoting humanistic religion and socialistic politics. "An arbitrator," he wrote once, "is one who examines both sides of a question and, after hearing all the evidence, makes a decision for one side. The examination of our civilization . . . has compelled the arbitrator [i.e., himself] to change from Nationalism to Internationalism, from Republicanism to Socialism, from Prudery to Realism, from Christianity to Humanism."[14]

Floyd pursued his own brand of humanism (or what he described as *scientific theology*) for several years before Unitarian religious humanism fully emerged. In the November 1925 issue of the *Arbitrator*, he carried a detailed explanation of this new religion that jibed almost completely with evolving religious humanism.[15] As a co-worker in many political causes with John Haynes Holmes,[16] Floyd was probably introduced to the Unitarian humanists through him.

By the time of his death in 1943, Floyd was fully affiliated with the American Humanist Association, leaving that organization much of his money in a last will and testament that began, "I, William Floyd, . . . disbelieving in the Lord God Jehovah and the Lord Jesus Christ, but believing in the highest ethical standards and the progress of the human race, being of sound mind and a humanist, do hereby . . ."

FRANK HANKINS (56), a native of Wilshire, Ohio, received his doctorate of philosophy from Columbia in 1908 and taught sociology at Clark University, the University of Pennsylvania, and Smith and Amherst Colleges. The president of the American Sociological Society (and a dedicated worker for population control), Hankins was a thorough-going evolutionary naturalist, who identified himself philosophically with the position of Roy Wood Sellars.

Publication of his book *Introduction to the Study of Society* gained Hankins a controversial reputation due to its chapter on "Myth, Magic, Religion, and Science," which offered a humanistic view of the topics.[17] Hankins never took the radical political or economic positions that some of his cosigners did and, while always deeply respected, was not a major figure in the propagation of the faith.

LLEWELYN JONES (48) was born in Great Britain and began his career as a reporter and editorial writer. He gradually worked his way up to the editorship of the Friday literary review of the *Chicago Evening Post*, an appointment he held from 1914–1932, and then became an editor with Willet, Clark, and Co. During these Chicago days, Jones taught writing and journalism at the University of Chicago and came into contact with religious humanism.

In 1938, Jones moved to Cambridge, Massachusetts, where he edited the *Christian Register* for three years. In addition, he lectured across the United States and delved into research and translation of Scandinavian literature, concentrating on the life and work of Bishop Gruntvig.[18]

ROBERT MORSE LOVETT (63) was a familiar figure among the educated left of the 1920s. A graduate of Harvard, he taught English for many years at the University of Chicago, where he also first became associated with humanism. His work on the editorial board of the *New Republic* (1922–1930) brought Lovett national attention. He was a renowned scholar and popular academic figure, whose signature added stature to the Manifesto, even though his contacts with the movement were largely tangential.

HAROLD PARSONS MARLEY (37) was the minister of Roy Wood Sellars's Ann Arbor Unitarian Church when the Manifesto was published in 1933. The son of a Kansas City merchandise broker (who died penniless), Marley grew up in the Disciples of Christ Church, of which Edward Scribners Ames, soon to be a distinguished scholar, was the minister.

After graduating from the University of Missouri, Marley enrolled at Union Theological Seminary and worked his way through school, getting caught up in the last strains of the Social Gospel and taking much inspiration from Harry Emerson Fosdick. By 1929, Marley's religious convictions had evolved beyond modernism, and he sought out Curtis W. Reese, who encouraged him to enter the Unitarian Church. Although Marley was a prolific author of short articles in Unitarian-associated journals, his interests focused upon the practical, rather than the philosophical or metaphysical.

This is not to say that Marley was without intellectual sophistication. While at Ann Arbor, he found that the atmosphere at the University of Michigan provided what he described as a "factory for the manufacture of humanism" with its constant debate and stimulation.[19] Both Sellars and Haydon, who spoke occasionally in Ann Arbor, shaped Marley's thinking until he could call himself a *conscientious humanist* and say, "There is hope for tomorrow. . . . [I]t is the hope of humanism which stirs the imagination of men who are beginning to realize that all this suffering might not have been. . . . It is the certainty that man can control his destiny, if he will."[20]

LESTER MONDALE (28) was one of the most independent forces in religious humanism. His father, a largely self-taught Minnesotan farmer-turned-Methodist minister, provided his children with an intense intellectual atmosphere that encouraged their searching out matters on their own. As a child, Mondale attended his father's three services each Sunday along with weekly prayer meetings and Bible study courses. This "overdose of religion" failed to abate during his undergraduate years at Hamline College in St. Paul, a Methodist institution that required attendance at three chapels a week.

By the middle of his college years, Mondale had discovered evolution (via his biology classes) and biblical criticism and had been
impressed by Andrew White's classic book, *History of the Warfare of
Science and Theology in Christendom* (1896). These intellectual ventures,
combined with the years of religious oversaturation he had experienced,
radically cooled Mondale's interest in religion until one Sunday he happened to be introduced to John Dietrich's First Unitarian Society in
Minneapolis. That day, Dietrich was talking about Immanuel Kant, and
the young Mondale was so impressed that, still skeptical, he returned
the next week to hear a sermon on Thomas Paine.

Mondale began attending Dietrich's church regularly, even recruit-
ing other students to accompany him. He was finally introduced to
Dietrich himself, whose first question to him was: "How would you like
to be a Unitarian minister?" Mondale was floored; he had never given
the idea any thought, having planned to be either a lawyer or a geolo-
gist. But in this church, the ministry combined the logic of law with
the science of geology. In short order, Dietrich arranged Mondale's
admittance to Harvard Divinity School, where he went in 1926, "100%
Dietrichian, an orthodox humanist!"[21]

Although Dietrich had provided Mondale with a philosophy with
which to integrate his thinking, the young theological student moved
slowly away from this rigidly naturalistic position over the next three
years and devoted the last year of his seminary career to a study of religious lives (under the direction of William Wallace Fenn). Mondale
wanted to know what religion did for people. To find an answer, he studied George Fox, John Wesley, St. Theresa, and others, only to discover
that people appeared to experience salvation when they were able to
overcome a sense of self-alienation and withdrawal from community
(the condition of a lost soul) and enter wholeheartedly into purposive
interaction with their sisters and brothers. These observations prompted
Mondale to declare Dietrich's exclusive emphasis upon science as a
means of salvation to be inadequate.

In addition to science, Mondale argued, people required personal
support, understanding, warmth, acceptance, and purpose. Here was
where the young minister broke with many of his humanist elders. His
disagreement did not result in disaffiliation, however. When Raymond
Bragg left Evanston to become secretary of the Western Unitarian Conference (WUC), Mondale succeeded him as minister of the Unitarian
Church in Evanston.

Upon walking into the WUC office one afternoon in 1933, Mondale was presented with the Manifesto and asked to sign. "I do so with reservations," he said, and that remark is reflective of his entire distinguished career. He was the youngest signer of the Humanist Manifesto, the only one who remains living as of the publication of this book, and, not incidentally, the stepbrother of former U.S. Vice-President Walter F. Mondale of Minnesota.

JOHN HERMAN RANDALL, JR. (34), was not involved in preparation of the Manifesto but did contribute to the *New Humanist* and was a rising star in philosophical circles. The son of a renowned philosopher, Randall took all his degrees from Columbia and taught there exclusively from 1925 until his retirement. He was a champion of Columbia's school of philosophical naturalism, and his two books, *The Making of the Modern Mind* (1926) and *Religion and the Modern World* (1929), were no doubt what first attracted religious humanists to him.

OLIVER REISER (37), another celebrated philosopher, was born in Columbus, Ohio, and educated at Ohio State. He spent his entire career teaching at the University of Pittsburgh (1926–1966). A highly original thinker, Reiser's interests were remarkably broad, ranging from the most complex speculative scientific philosophy to Eastern thought, from psychic research to the United Nations satellite systems.[22] Even though he published a number of significant books for humanism (including *Humanistic Logic* [1930] and *The Promise of Scientific Humanism* [1940]) and was highly influenced by John Dewey, Reiser was something of a maverick. Toward the end of his career, he underwent a change in thinking that moved him closer to a kind of complex theism, which he described in his last two major books, *Man's New Image of Man* (1961) and *Cosmic Humanism* (1966).

Reiser's thought in this period was virtually unintelligible to a lay reader, so complex was his attempt to fashion a new cosmic theory. What is plain, however, is that he reverted to theistic language, arguing, for example, that "God is man's name for the Guiding Field or Cosmic Imagination by means of which differentiated energy is focused in nodal points in space-time, subsequently to evolve under the influence of guiding fields on higher levels"[23] and providing in *Cosmic Humanism* for an "unmanifest realm" for divinity. Here was a powerful and creative mind at work and, beyond that, a truly honest man. When asked to elaborate upon some of the complexities in his latest book (*Cosmic Humanism*), Reiser remarked, "I am beginning to think the author himself knows little about his subject!"[24]

CLINTON LEE SCOTT (age unknown), the only Universalist to sign the Manifesto, was the tenth of twelve children born to a Canadian couple who moved to a farm in Vermont when Scott was a child. His father, "a farmer who liked fast horses," was an Anglican "but never worked at it much"; he died when Scott was nine. His mother, a college graduate who had taught school before she married, was probably, in her son's words, "a humanist without knowing it"; she, too, died early, when Scott was fourteen.

As a youngster, Scott attended the Free Will Baptist Church Sunday school, but several incidents of hypocrisy associated with that experience shaped his early rebellion against orthodoxy. The first concerned a Sunday school teacher, Mr. Rogers, who instructed the youngster that the "golden text" for one Sunday—"He who calleth his brother a fool shall be in danger of hellfire"—meant exactly what it said. "It so happened," recalled Scott years later, "that the word *fool* was probably the most frequently used in my vocabulary, . . . so I tried courageously to eliminate [its use] . . . and with some success." The next week, however, Scott and a friend happened to see Rogers on the road, and one of the boys pretended to wave his hands in Rogers's horse's face, startling the horse and eliciting from an angry Rogers the cry, "You fool!" "From that day on," explained Scott, "I could never think of Rogers except as a hypocrite. . . . He was probably a good man but he had a bad religion."[25]

Another crucial incident involved a Sunday school teacher who asked the class, "Now how many of you, when you think of how good God is, go to the barn and pray your thanks to Him?" Each of the children asserted that they did so often, even though they were lying, and when Scott was asked, he told the truth. "No, ma'am," he said. "Never." After the teacher spent the remainder of the day upbraiding him for his godlessness, Scott vowed never to return to church.

When he was in preparatory school, however, Scott and a friend were offered the chance to earn some money pumping the organ for two local congregations. The young men jumped at the opportunity and, neither caring which church they served, flipped coins to decide. Scott won the Universalist Church and was mightily impressed to hear enlightened Universalist teaching (in particular, that the Old Testament was not the word of God but the mythology of the Jewish people).

Within a short time, Scott had given up his notions of becoming a lawyer and entered Tufts University to study for the ministry. From 1915–1925, he retained a broadly theistic perspective but was influenced to move in a humanistic direction after his contacts with two individuals: A. Eustace Haydon, with whom Scott studied sociology briefly at the University of Chicago, and E. Burdette Backus, who in 1925 was minister of the Unitarian Church in Los Angeles while Scott was minister of the Universalist. Tiring of trying to explain the contradiction between a benevolent God and a world full of evil, Scott soon embraced humanism fully (although his was of a more mystical variety).

With his call to the Universalist Church in Peoria, Illinois, in the late 1920s, Scott became active in the Western Unitarian Conference (WUC), speaking frequently at Unitarian meetings. It was by this route that he was introduced to Raymond Bragg, Edwin H. Wilson, Curtis W. Reese, and their associates and subsequently asked to sign the Manifesto. Even though he was criticized by his fellow Universalists (who were always a bit more conservative than the Unitarians), he was generally accorded eminence and respect, for Scott's religion grew up out of his experience ("I was never too impressed by what I read in books") and was manifested in his daily life.[26]

ROY WOOD SELLARS (age unknown), the principal author of the Manifesto, was born in Canada but raised in a small, "almost pioneer community in northeastern Michigan." He was the son of a struggling country doctor who "was almost a zealot in his insistence upon education." Sellars recalled later, "I arrived at the University of Michigan at the age of nineteen, an undoubtedly queer freshman, with a large amount of self-education mingled with my schooling."[27] He received his doctorate of philosophy from that institution in 1908 and remained on its faculty throughout his career.

G. E. Moore's neorealism, William James's *Principles of Psychology* (1890), and philosophical pragmatism all contributed to the development of Sellars's thought, but he was always an independent spirit:

> [M]y general outlook has been dominated by the set of my own personality, which is strongly self-conscious and individualistic. . . . I have always rejected any theory which did not do justice to the uniqueness of each center of consciousness. . . . Thus, while in sympathy with the general fight of pragmatism against absolute idealism, I could never accept the tendency of the Chicago school to a social consciousness.[28]

MAYNARD SHIPLEY (60) was born in Baltimore, Maryland. He attended Stanford University for two years but never received a degree. Nevertheless, he was fascinated by all matters scientific and developed an expertise in the popular appreciation and presentation of science. In 1898, he founded the Seattle Academy of Science and, in 1924, started the Science League of America, a national association to protect freedom in teaching and to resist attempts to unite church and state in the United States.

A popular public and radio lecturer on astronomy and evolution, Shipley's two books, *The War on Modern Science* (1927) and *The Key to Evolution* (1929), no doubt attracted the humanists' attention. Even so, Shipley was but a fringe person in the larger movement. He lived only a short time after signing the Manifesto, dying in June 1934.

W. FRANK SWIFT (32) was born in Wigon, England. He graduated from Meadville in 1928, one of the younger generation of humanists, with a thesis—"Neohumanism as a Religious Philosophy"—that drew heavily upon the humanist "saints": John Dietrich, Frank C. Doan, A. Eustace Haydon, Joseph Wood Krutch, John Herman Randall, Jr., Curtis W. Reese, and A. Wakefield Slaten. In concluding that paper, Swift wrote,

> Far from being "cold" the Neohumanist feels that his philosophy is warm with the glow of human feeling. . . . And "pessimistic"? On the contrary, the Neohumanist is the most incorrigible optimist, for he is able to look at the real facts of life squarely and unflinchingly; and in the face of hard—and often uncomforting—truth is able to build a religious philosophy at once both hopeful and satisfying.[29]

Following his graduation, Swift became associate leader of the St. Louis Ethical Society (1928–1930) and then entered into educational and research work in New York City and Boston. He was tragically killed in an auto accident in December 1933, only six months after signing the Manifesto.[30]

VIVIAN T. THAYER (47) was the Nebraska-born, Wisconsin-raised son of a Methodist minister. His father came gradually to be identified with the more liberal wing of the Methodist Church and, near the end of his life, was considered something of a skeptic by his disapproving Methodist colleagues. This spirit of doubt surely influenced the young Thayer, who left home at age thirteen. His mother had died when he was four, and his father had grown increasingly unable to support the family. The young man supported himself through secondary school at Carroll

College and through undergraduate and graduate years at the University of Wisconsin.

Perhaps Thayer's earliest acquaintance with systematic unbelief came with his discovery of Ingersoll late in his secondary years, but it was Max Otto, more than anyone else, who shaped this humanist's thinking. Roommates for several years, Otto and Thayer shared their lives and thoughts, and as Otto moved toward a pragmatic position in philosophy, Thayer followed. After serving several years in the school system of Ashland, Wisconsin, Thayer returned to the university to take his doctorate in philosophy (with a dissertation on Spinoza) and to teach briefly at Madison. In 1922, however, he accepted an invitation to become the principal of the Ethical Culture High School in New York, and from 1928–1948, he served as educational director of all Ethical Culture schools.

Thayer had been introduced to humanism by Otto and A. Eustace Haydon, who had served for a time as pulpit supply for the Madison Unitarian Church. But it was not until 1932 that Thayer had contact with the Chicago humanists. His contributions to humanism, therefore, were largely post-Manifesto and took the form of frequent publications in the *Humanist* as well as a practical witness to humanist ideals in all his educational commitments.[31]

ELDRED CORNELIUS VANDERLAAN (43) was born in Muskegon, Michigan. He attended Hope College in Holland, Michigan, before entering the ministry of the Reformed Church. He was educated at Union Theological School in New York City, where he received his doctorate of theology in 1924 and was a protege of liberal theologian A. C. McGiffert. Vanderlaan served Reformed churches in New York State before entering the Unitarian ministry in 1926 as minister of the First Unitarian Church of Berkeley, California. The author of a book entitled *Fundamentalism vs. Modernism*, Vanderlaan resigned the ministry of the Berkeley church in late 1932 to become leader of the Free Fellowship, a humanist group in Berkeley. He remained in that position at the time of the Manifesto's publication.[32]

JOSEPH WALKER (67) was one of the most unusual humanists. He was a patrician New Englander, was educated at Brown and Harvard Universities, served as one-time Republican candidate for governor of Massachusetts, and completed two years as speaker of the Massachusetts House of Representatives—not credentials usually associated with a humanist.

By the early 1930s, however, Walker had arrived at a largely humanist religious perspective and had done so independent of the common sources of the formal movement. He set forth his views on "a sound philosophy of life and a religion without supernaturalism or superstition" for the benefit of his wife and children, and hearing of John Dietrich's compatible views, he sent a copy to the Minneapolis minister. "By all means, publish this," encouraged Dietrich, and Walker's *Humanism as a Way of Life* appeared in 1932. Said the former politician, "God, for me, . . . is a pure Ideal, created by the mind and imagination of man and existing, only as an Ideal, in the minds and hearts of men. . . . Religion, for me, . . . is the love and devotion to the best within us, that is, the Ideal."[33]

Albert C. Dieffenbach arranged Walker's signing of the Manifesto, and although Walker played a minor role in the developing movement, his name added prestige and diversity to the list of signers.

RABBI JACOB J. WEINSTEIN (30), a native of Poland, came to the United States at the age of five but was not naturalized for another eighteen years. A student at Reed College and Hebrew Union, Weinstein was ordained in 1929 and served synagogues in Austin, Texas, and San Francisco before becoming advisor to Jewish students at Columbia in 1932. Before completing his career in Chicago (1939–1970), Weinstein directed Jewish adult studies in New York City and San Francisco.

FRANK SCOTT COREY WICKS (65), a Congregationalist by birth and the son of a Millville, Massachusetts, woolen manufacturer, was one of the "grand old men" of religious humanism, even in 1933. The minister of All Souls Church in Indianapolis (he had previously served Unitarian churches in Passaic, New Jersey, and Brighton and Malden, Massachusetts), Wicks had been one of the first established ministers to endorse the new religious perspective.

Wicks was never a scholar; in fact, he remarked that, for a time, he simply reworked A. Wakefield Slaten's sermons and used them as his own. Nonetheless, Wicks's essay "Good Men in Hell" went through thirty-three printings between 1914 and 1943 and was distributed nationally by the American Unitarian Association.[34] Another of Wicks's contributions was a "Humanistic Decalogue" to replace the Ten Commandments; this unpublished paper began, "Thou shalt worship all Truth, Goodness, Beauty as manifest in Human Life, and accept no person in lieu thereof." This gentle minister retired in 1938 and died in 1952.

DAVID RHYS WILLIAMS (43) was perhaps the most theologically (although certainly not politically) conservative signer of the Manifesto. Born in Keane Valley, New York, he was the son and grandson of Congregationalist ministers. As a teenager, Williams had been impressed by the life story of evangelist Dwight Moody and was moved to enter the ministry. But before he had completed his education—first at Marietta College and then at Harvard Divinity School—"the whole superstructure of beliefs" about religion that had been his since childhood collapsed around him, due largely to the influence of a book by English agnostic Robert Blatchford.

Williams may have lost his theology, but his social commitment remained strong. He was, in fact, one of the leading social activists of the Unitarian ministry in the first half of the twentieth century. "When I began my ministry," he wrote years later, "I possessed no theology worthy of the name. . . . I continued to have a vague belief in Deity, but I was at a loss to explain my belief."[35] The first eleven years of that ministry were spent in joint Congregational-Unitarian fellowship, but Williams served only Congregational churches. Not until 1924, when he was called to the Third Unitarian Church of Chicago, did he take a Unitarian settlement. He remained in that denomination the rest of his life.

No doubt, the political values the Manifesto endorsed were largely what first attracted Williams to the document. In addition, he experienced some lack of clarity as to just what humanism implied theologically. Within six months of the issuance of the Manifesto, he was embroiled in a theological controversy with Roy Wood Sellars in the pages of the *Register*. "As one of the sponsors of the Manifesto," Williams wrote in November 1933, under the title "Humanism and Mysticism," "I think I am correct in saying [that humanism does not] necessarily rule out faith in an indwelling God whose power and presence can be substantiated by the facts of man's mystical experiences."[36] Quick to reply, Sellars labeled Williams's view "a forced view which is unique with him, and not shared with the other signers." Sellars went on to challenge Williams's position and to ask what mode of existence this indwelling God might have. And then he ridiculed the tendency to make abstractions like power, life, energy, and ideal into God: "To the modern technical philosopher [he went on] modernistic religious literature is a series of capital letters, and he is . . . convinced that Comte was right when he identified metaphysics with the deification of abstractions."[37]

By the 1960s Williams's break with humanism was complete, and he published a book entitled *Faith Beyond Humanism* (1963) to atone for his earlier indiscretions.

EDWIN HENRY WILSON (34) was the most ardent publicist of religious humanism for more than forty years. Raised in Concord, Massachusetts, he was baptized and religiously educated by the First Parish Church (Unitarian) of that town. His father—who, at one time or another, sold fruit, built houses, and farmed—had no more than a high school education but was an inveterate reader; he had little use for the church, however. Wilson's mother, the daughter of a Methodist minister, was the cousin of Charles E. St. John, secretary of the American Unitarian Association (which is the equivalent of being president today). It was through his mother that Wilson was introduced to Unitarianism.

The First Parish in Concord was a typical conservative church of the day, and Wilson considered himself an Emersonian theist. (Ralph Waldo Emerson's essay on "Self-Reliance" had been important to him.) At the time, he was asked to supervise a high school youth group in Second Church, Boston. And while he had been headed for a career in business (having earned a business degree from Boston University), his contacts with youth and their persistent questions about religious matters encouraged him to go into the ministry. In that profession, he thought, he might be able to end the cycle of ignorance that was passed from one generation to another.

In 1924, Wilson he set out for Meadville Theological School in Allegheny, Pennsylvania. Before he left, however, his Aunt Martha (St. John's wife) warned him, "Don't let those humanists at Meadville take away your faith!" In fact, it was not the Meadville humanists but a philosophy professor whom Wilson met on the train to Pennsylvania who first moved him in the humanist direction. Upon hearing that this young man was headed to theological school, the professor expressed regret that such a bright person would be throwing away his life in a profession grounded on such false premises. This conversation confirmed Wilson's doubts about theism, and in a short while (thanks largely to his acquaintance with the works of Auguste Comte, Roy Wood Sellars, and Curtis W. Reese), he proclaimed himself a humanist.

Upon graduation from Meadville, Wilson spent a year abroad as a Cruft Fellow at Manchester College in Oxford, England, and then took up the ministry of the First Unitarian Church in Dayton, Ohio. By 1933, he had left Dayton for Chicago and was deeply immersed in the propagation of the humanist faith, a commitment that would lead him to take large parts in the formation of the American Humanist Association and the Fellowship of Religious Humanists. For many years, he edited the *Humanist* magazine, which was the successor to the *New Humanist*.[38]

# The Philosophy of Religious Humanism

Religious humanism, while it self-consciously understood itself to be a religion, was grounded in philosophy. More specifically, it was, in large measure, an amalgamation of two closely related philosophical schools: *pragmatism* (or *instrumentalism*) and *critical realism*. The child of the union was something that might best be labeled *evolutionary naturalism* (at least, that was Roy Wood Sellars's name for it).

This appendix will first sketch the pragmatic heritage, as it culminated in the work of John Dewey; then move into a broad view of the philosophy of religious humanism, as it applied to the nature of humans and the cosmos and of religion and ethics; and conclude with a description of the views of Sellars, humanism's principal philosopher, author of the Manifesto, and the man in whose thought the philosophy of early religious humanism is embodied in its most intellectually sophisticated form.

## The Pragmatic Heritage

The source of pragmatism was the great Prussian G. W. F. Hegel. From Hegel come two critical notions requisite to an appreciation of pragmatism: (1) the idea that truth might be seen as developmental, in some sense, and (2) the conviction that reality and experience constitute an organic whole composed of interrelated entities within a natural context. With these two principles in mind, it is useful to consider pragmatisms's philosophical triumvirate, starting with the renowned American philosopher/psychologist William James and proceeding to F. C. S. Schiller and then John Dewey.

In 1890, William James published *Principles of Psychology*,[1] which was to have a significant impact upon philosophical thought for the next three decades. Consciousness, said James in a radical challenge to the then prevailing understanding of the term, is a steady flow of ideas, perceptions, and relations, and those relations are as much a part of the human experience as the objects being related. Human consciousness plays a large part in establishing the relationships between entities throughout the universe, as Hegel insisted. Joseph L. Blau makes clear the implications of this view: "We do not need to import, . . . either from the realm of the supernatural or from the transcendent nature of the mind itself [a reference to Kantian idealism], an explanation of the connectedness of the universe of our experience."[2] That connectedness is, in part, derived from the nature of consciousness itself. This is the first step toward establishing the primacy of the human over the divine and the efficacy of human experience as a determinant of reality. It would be the human mind, not the power of God, for example, that "held it all together," where *it* referred to (our perception of) the universe.

James's major legacy was his theory of knowledge and truth, something not unrelated to his definition of consciousness. Convinced of the importance of consciousness in delineating reality, James proposed that although the meaning of a statement is deduced by examining its consequences, the public verifiability of those consequences is not as important as the use to which we put that statement. What concrete difference will believing one statement as opposed to another make in our lives? If doing so has led us to achieve results that we expected and consider good, then it is true; if not, it is false. The criterion for labeling a contention true or false is what happens with that contention in the future. If we can assimilate it into our experience, if it helps us reach a new and satisfactory relationship with some other part of our experience, then it may be called true. "The truth of an idea is not a stagnant property inherent in it," claimed James. "Truth *happens* to an idea. It *becomes* true, is *made* true by events."[3]

Truth does not have to agree with reality; on the contrary, like Hegel, James assures us that our experience of truth *is* the reality. If our judgments of truth or falsehood are based upon our experience of concrete differences in our lives, then that experience has to be the reality. But remember, truth is experienced not at the moment it is verbalized but in the future, as its consequences are realized. In this sense, truth is, for James, developmental.

The result of such theorizing for religious belief is monumental. As James argues, "If theological ideas prove to have a value, . . . they will be true for pragmatism, in the sense of being good for so much. For how much more they will be true will depend entirely on their relations to the other truths that also have to be acknowledged."[4]

Indeed, if there is no intellectual reason to reject a religious proposition, then we have a right to choose the option that will have the most satisfactory consequences in our lives. But we cannot believe anything that contradicts or violates other truths we hold. We must be self-consistent. Those ideas are true that have the greatest staying power, but since any such truth may eventually be replaced, our truths will always be in flux. Nevertheless, as James says in his famous essay "The Will to Believe," [W]e have the right to believe at our own risk any hypothesis which is live enough to tempt our will [for a time]."[5]

James wants to convince us that, whether we like it or not, this description of how we decide upon the value of any particular truth corresponds to how we all make decisions about truth. If we believe something provides the most efficacious way to achieve some desired end and if that idea is consistent with our basic presuppositions, we will believe it and call it *true*. How much more dynamic a view of truth could one ask for?

The relevance of this epistemology to the humanists is not in its specific avowals but in its vision of truth as nonstatic, consequential, and replaceable—all characteristics that empiricism requires. Moreover, its preoccupation with human knowing, its conviction that the process of knowing affects the known, and its postulate of an organically interrelated universe are all relevant to basic humanist thought.[6]

Englishman F. C. S. Schiller was a pragmatist by philosophy and a humanist by title (although hardly a religious humanist). A review of the core of Schiller's thinking reveals several familiar points. For instance, Schiller was convinced that

> all acts and thoughts are unreducibly the products of individual human beings and are therefore inescapably colored by the needs, desires, and purposes of men. What we call knowledge, hence, is a growing and varying thing. It evolves. . . . The logic we use is not eternally fixed and absolute, but dynamic and changing. Man makes his truth. . . . Axioms are not God-given, but man-made. . . . [P]ostulates are working hypotheses, whose truth grows or diminishes in our experience.[7]

The only way to know the truth of a statement, Schiller asserted, is to test it, and the only way to test it is to see it in application. Abstract truths are unemployable and useless. In order to be confident that we understand an idea correctly, we need to ask what the purpose behind the statement is and what need its utterance will fulfill. To this point and in his acknowledgment of a "right to postulate" in those areas where issues are still open, Schiller appears hardly distinguishable from James.

But in one area—the explicit enunciation of pragmatism's doctrine of human nature (or what Schiller called *humanism's* doctrine of human nature)—the English philosopher went beyond James and anticipated the religious humanists in a striking fashion some twenty-five years before they appeared on the scene. Humanism, he proclaimed, "demands that man's integral nature shall be used as the whole premise which philosophy must argue from wholeheartedly, that man's complete satisfaction shall be the conclusion philosophy must aim at, that philosophy shall not cut itself loose from the real problems of life by making initial abstractions which are false."8 And in another place, he described humanism as "[t]he philosophical attitude which, without wasting thought upon attempts to construct experience *a priori*, is content to take human experience, content to take man on his own merits, just as he is to start with . . . to remember that an ultimate philosophy which analyzes us away is thereby merely exhibiting its failure to achieve its purpose."9

Suspicious of abstractions, Schiller criticized metaphysics as being "imaginative and conjectural" and hardly meeting the pragmatic test of utility. And in a final grand forecast of evolutionary naturalism, Schiller called for a "valid metaphysic" that can "be built up piecemeal bit by bit, by the discovery that truths which have been found useful in the sciences may be advantageously taken as ultimate and combined into a more and more harmonious system."10

James and Schiller provided much of the philosophical background out of which religious humanism grew, but it was in John Dewey that the humanists found their most direct inspiration. If the world were an ideal place and all absolute truth was known absolutely, Dewey's philosophy would never have come into being. But the world was far from ideal in the early twentieth century, and the preeminence of absolutism had dissipated, largely in the face of scientific and evolutionary developments. Thus, the world was a very real place with very real problems.

Dewey had absorbed from William James the idea that what we choose to believe and know must somehow be related to the consequences of those beliefs. Confronted with overwhelming problems, humans had discovered a tool for eliminating at least a few of those problems: the sciences. The consequences of believing in the scientific process had been, in some cases, encouraging.

But what exactly was the relationship between the believing and the consequences? The latter did not spring spontaneously and mystically from the former. Between the two poles lay Schiller's application or, as Dewey phrased it, *instrumental experimentation*. In Dewey's mind, knowledge and action were not segregated; in fact, knowledge without action was not really knowledge at all. Dewey maintained that ideas—whether of a scientific or common day-to-day variety—are proposals for action.

Because no one possesses all knowledge, we are regularly confronted with situations of doubt. Thinking begins in the midst of a doubtful situation and aims to remove that doubt. Knowledge, for Dewey, is the process by which we first evaluate that doubtful situation, formulate possible solutions (ideas), and proceed to verify our solutions experimentally. Ideas, then, are proposals for action that may be employed to satisfy a doubtful situation by removing the doubt.

All those variables that affect one's knowing—physical perspective, social and cultural history, and so on—come to bear not only upon *how* we know but also upon *what* we know. Knowing is a process, not a finalizable achievement. And it is a process that parallels the process of scientific inquiry: a process of hypothesis (proposal for action), experimentation, and temporary verification (which is always subject to reevaluation). There is no longer a rigid dichotomy between the experience and the experiencer. We interact with the world. Appearance and reality have much in common, since our knowing (as problem solving) plays a part in the construction of that reality. Dewey puts it this way: "Experience denotes what is experienced, the world caught up into experiencing. Nature's place in man is no less significant than man's place in nature [Hegelian interconnectedness.] . . . The fact of integration in life is a basic fact."[11]

Once we rid ourselves of the debilitating quest for certainty—giving up the quest of the ages to construct the Truth or the Good—we may turn to our major resource: intelligence. Intelligence may intrude itself into that complicated conglomeration of interactions we call Nature and may actively direct changes in the course of events.

Dewey's understanding of intelligence has been defined as "the operation of the vast stream of experience at the conscious and responsible level."[12] Human intelligence, coupled with the empirical method and technological resources, is in a position to literally remake the world. Very little about the conditions of our existence need any longer be taken for granted. Truth and reality have been vanquished. Problems have taken the place of reality, and developmental knowledge has taken the place of truth. An idea (as a proposal for action) is no longer so much true or false as it is effective or ineffective (that is, instrumental) in solving a problem.

To the religious humanists, the notion that human intelligence (via the experimental method) might break down fixed patterns and induce change was an exciting one. It meant, among other things, that ideals were no longer billowy abstractions but might be the very stuff with which to redo the world. To intellectuals like the humanists, this was a delicious possibility. Dewey applied the word *real* to "that which has to be accepted as the material of change, as the obstructions and the means of certain specific desired changes. . . . [T]he ideal . . . represents intelligently thought-out possibilities of the existent world which may be used as methods for making over and improving it."[13]

Here, the role of intelligence in the change process is clear. By conceiving of ideals in this fashion and intervening methodically and responsibly in natural events, we may help to bring about the kind of world we desire. But we may also destroy our world. This is the very nature of human experience. Because nothing is preordained or directed by a supraintelligent entity, everything is left to us. And the results may be affirmative or disastrous.

This notion is exactly what Dewey installed at the heart of his reconception of the religious. God, he argued, is the active relation between ideal ends and actual conditions; the religious attitude is one of reverence for the union of these two forms, a union that takes place only when humans are no longer isolated from their environment but rather take part in it, interact with it intelligently. That such a union may come to be in this fashion is the basis of Deweyan religious faith.[14]

Beneath this theory of knowledge and action lies a theory of humans and the cosmos. The Deweyan universe is the scientific universe: It is real; it is open; it is infinite. Change is omnipresent with or without human beings (although it is clear how we humans may intervene effectively to induce change). The doctrine of final causes and fixed ends that the theologians and the teleological philosophers hold to is dismissed. The world is malleable; its ends are not fixed and we are potent forces in its recreation. "Nature is subdued to human purpose,"

Dewey allowed, "because it is no longer the slave of metaphysical and theological purpose." Matter is no longer atomistic, staid, and impenetrable; rather, it comprises the conditions that either hinder or further the attainment of some end—it comprises the conditions of human achievement. Organization in matter and the universe is self-existing. As Dewey suggested, "Experience carries principles of connection and organization within itself,"[15] rendering supernatural interference unnecessary.

Coming as Dewey's philosophy did, on the explosive heels of the technological revolution, it readily reinforced the conviction already spreading for several decades (since Huxley's time and before) that science could transform being. Humans were flexing their muscles in Nature's face; intelligence, judgment, and scientific input could regulate and direct Nature. Lacking the obstacle a deity might provide and confident that the universe (matter) was waiting to be exploited for human benefit, humanity stood in awe before the possibilities. Religious humanism institutionalized that awe.

## Humanism Emergent

Humanist thought and the philosophy of religious humanism can be reviewed against the backdrop of Dewey's theories of knowledge and action and his philosophy of the religious.

As primitive humans encountered the world, announced A. Eustace Haydon, they found it complex and threatening. And so, the eternal quest of the ages has been the desire to erect a safe, satisfying way of living on earth. But at some point, humans were confronted with the fact of failure and turned to a compensatory world of wishes and ideals, transferring the responsibility for attaining a better life on earth from their own shoulders to the realm of a superpersonal absolute. They have been plagued ever since by the dualism between the world of humans (and matter) and the sphere of God (and the ideal absolute).[16]

Humanism reacted against this artificial world of metaphysical separation. It argued that the world of the supernatural and absolute must be rejected, not only because it fails to square with the facts that science reveals but also because it makes humanity feel helpless, impotent, and irresponsible before the world and its future. (As the fifth and sixth points of the Manifesto put it, "Humanism asserts that the nature of the universe depicted by modern science makes unacceptable any supernatural or cosmic guarantees of human values" and "We are convinced that the time has passed for theism.") Rejecting the notion that an intelligent will influences human fortune, the humanists were left with a choice between a mechanistic (materialistic, atomistic) view of the universe and a naturalistic view. Almost without exception, they chose the latter.[17] "Materialism or, as it was known in its lower stages, atomism," wrote Curtis W. Reese, "levels man downward, and constantly looks with suspicion upon all that is not explainable by the locomotion of materials."[18] To a group of people imbued with the Deweyan bias toward the efficacy of human intelligence, such a philosophy of blind, hard, purposeless atomism would never do.

The humanists hardly denied that the universe was independent of humanity and entirely self-sufficient. (The first point of the Manifesto states, "Religious humanists regard the universe as self-existing.") But they saw in it the nurturance of humans, as well. At the least, they recognized the world to be orderly and stable, not given to radical discontinuities. Sacrificing the mechanistic predisposition, Max Otto turned to a scientific naturalism, in which humanity and nature coexisted interdependently: "Man in his total being is looked upon as an electron-proton system, interrelated with any number of other aggregates, all of which taken together, constitute the universe."[19] ("Humanism believes that man is a part of nature and that he has emerged as the result of a continuous process," reads the second point of the Manifesto.)

But what did humans have to go on, situated, as they were, in the midst of a vast and effectively neutral universe, unaided by divine assurance or a realm of the ideal essence? Well, in the first place, the universe extended its own corrective in the form of the evolutionary impulse, which, over thousands of years, gradually reshaped the world, presumably for the better. By encouraging the development of higher levels of complex organization, nature supplied a powerful thrust, which humans might choose to label "good" or describe as an "improvement," as it struck them.

Even though the evolutionary process might provide some comfort, it was a slow, hardly noticeable process that failed to satisfy the religious urges of dissatisfied people. If nature and evolution could not be counted on to underwrite cosmological achievement (at least, not at an adequate pace), the only alternative was human beings. Humanists believed that humans might speed up the slow processes of nature.[20]

And indeed, humans did have the means to encourage those processes. Haydon suggested that science would provide security where the sacred had before. Dewey assured his followers that human intelligence could influence natural events: The world was not complete and finished; humanity could have a part in the process of its making. And what would be the best way to take advantage of that participation? Max Otto said,

> The most liveable life must be sought and found in the physical environment which conditions our efforts and which . . . is indifferent to our success or failure. . . . Nature, then, is to be utilized. But to utilize nature, we must study nature and scientific method is the best means . . . for that task. . . . Science [is] man's effort to master the facts of nature and to discover the best means for drawing upon nature's resources.[21]

But the acquisition of facts was not enough. The Deweyan model of knowledge must be carried through. Facts must be hinged to action. Accumulated scientific data must be employed experimentally. The formula for recreating human existence, urged Reese in a self-conscious adaptation of Dewey, was to observe and experience and then to incorporate those calculations into regulated experimental living. "The ideal grows out of real experience," he wrote. "It is consciously tested and re-made in the light of new facts."[22]

And what was that ideal, that highest value? The full development of human personality. Little else of comparable value can be found within the universe; most humanists would say *nothing* else. (As stated in the eighth point of the Manifesto, "Religious humanism considers the complete realization of human personality to be the end of man's life and seeks its development and fulfillment in the here and now.") That is the religious task, and science is the means. Such a perspective clearly alters the relationship between human beings and nature. The two now constitute a unity that, according to Reese, "occurs because its components constantly come into relation and interaction with each other, rather than a unity which pre-exists and produces the relations and interactions."[23]

In a relationship of this sort, humans may take advantage of the consistency of natural law to make their dreams real. Natural laws can be used, for example, to predict the behavior of people and things and to provide the security that genuine freedom and human growth require. As Reese noted, "Somehow and to some extent the cosmic situation conditions but does not regulate human development."[24] Science in no way hinders human development but supports it. Yet science is no more than a tool and a method, one which, as some humanists warned, might be misused. It needed something more; it needed the guidance that religion and ethics might provide.

When humans recognized they could be effective agents in determining the future, they also realized that they would need a philosophy to support and guide them. That philosophy—as Dewey first articulated—needed to be grounded in human experience. "The great gift which we may expect from philosophy," wrote J. A. C. Fagginner Auer, "is a method which will serve us in handling the facts of life."[25] But what philosophy should we choose, and what role will it play in the fulfillment of our ideals?

In the first place, the philosophy must be rooted deep in a conviction of intrinsic human worth. Reese refused to allow human beings to be treated as a means to any other end than their own growth. "Whatever purposes . . . the cosmos is working out, man is not to be regarded as a means for their realization," he proclaimed.[26] Humans are valuable, in and of themselves. Their nature is malleable, and they are the only creatures who may proceed to change themselves by their own will after critical self-examination. Human nature is not originally depraved, as orthodox Christianity would have it, but simply unorganized and undirected. As Reese put it, "Conflicts in the impulsive life are abnormalities due to the misunderstanding and misuse of the impulses. The well-balanced, fully-developed and intelligently controlled impulsive life is the full life."[27]

Humans in a civilized condition, then, are constructive agents for social advance. And social advance, the development of personality, the construction of the ideal livable life—these are the goals of the religious person. The quest of modern women and men is no different from that of early humans. ("[T]he humanist finds his religious emotions expressed in a heightened sense of personal life and in a cooperative effort to promote social well-being," proclaims the ninth point of the Manifesto.) But now, people have the advantage of having empiricism at their disposal. Religion, like Deweyan knowledge, now takes the form of a problem-solving apparatus. Haydon put this succinctly: "The purposive use of this factual knowledge for the release and fulfillment of human potentialities is, in practice, the meaning of modern religion."[28]

It was little wonder, then, that humanism, as a religious force, was constantly coupled with calls for social and economic reform. There was, in the humanist view, simply no distinction between religious and social affairs. All fell under the rubric of human engagement (As the seventh point of the Manifesto states, "Religion consists of those actions, purposes, and experiences which are humanly significant. . . . It includes labor, art, science, philosophy, love, recreation. . . . Religious humanism maintains that all associations and institutions exist for the fulfillment of human life. The intelligent evaluation, transformation, control, and direction of such associations and institutions with a view to the enhancement of human life is the purpose and program of humanism.")

Dewey argued in *Human Nature and Conduct* that the type of society influences the kind of idealism dominantly chosen within it.[29] If we change society, we alter its ideals (goals), as well. The good life depends upon the good society. This follows quite logically from the assumption of interconnectedness that pervades humanist thought. Religion must address itself to the reorganizing of the social structure. Haydon would have such a new society "mold material to the service of life, make machines lift the load of labor from man's shoulders, . . . lift civilization into forms of cultural beauty."[30] Oliver Reiser would have humanists think in terms of a "United States of the World, implemented with police powers to enforce common decisions. . . . Global planning . . . is a next step in the utilization of our social intelligence."[31] Otto was outspoken in his calls for economic socialism, and Reese noted that humanism recognized the priority of personal rights over property rights and stressed the interdependence of people and the desirability of a planned and controlled economy.[32]

Religious humanism of the 1930s was tied intimately to the popular movements of social restructuring. The effort to erect a free and just social order was integral to humanistic religiosity. And that effort formed the basis of the humanists' ethical system, as well. For them, human ethics were experimental, not fixed; a free person must act in accordance with his or her intellect. Values should be loved and clung to, not for their own sakes but only to the extent that they contribute to human well-being. Dewey had taught the humanists that

> [a] moral law . . . is not something to swear by and stick to at all hazards; it is a formula of the way to respond when specific conditions present themselves. Its soundness and pertinence are tested by what happens when it is acted upon. Its claim or authority rests finally upon the imperativeness of the situation that has to be dealt with, not upon its own intrinsic value.[33]

And so, the humanists stressed the autonomy of an individual's will to make judgments that follow from the application of human intelligence. Much physical and social evil could be vanquished by the unselfish use of scientific resources. "Evil is a fact of protean form," intoned Haydon, "to be met by understanding through analysis and, in the light of ideal adjustment, if possible, overcome."[34] It was a fine suggestion where physical suffering was concerned, but it was hardly helpful as a solution to the maze of moral quandaries with which human beings have always been confronted. But then, humanism did not pretend to offer pat, creedal answers to anything.

It is difficult to represent the humanists' position more specifically for the very reason that they shunned dogma and, as disciples of the scientific mode, were conditioned to be open to change and reevaluation. In many respects, this frame of reference probably stimulated in them a tolerance and inclusiveness that other philosophical/religious fellowships lacked. But it also made them harder to pin down on some concrete issues. Evolution, by its very nature, means that human ideas cannot be final or absolute; the humanists allowed for the possibility that they might change their minds on a given subject over time. Then, too, they were a group of self-respecting individualists, never chary of entering into conflict with each other. Their first principles stood, however, pretty much as outlined here.

Humanism owes an enormous intellectual debt to pragmatism, particularly the Deweyan brand. Reiser's words may put the case most sharply. Humanism took from pragmatism, he said, the notions that "the world is still incomplete, still in the making, and that man is a real agent in determining the character and direction of developments yet to come."[35] But there were other influences, as well, and none were more important than the *critical realism* of the preeminent religious humanist thinker, Roy Wood Sellars of the University of Michigan.

## The Manifesto's Philosopher

Sellars was an advocate of a new epistemology called *neorealism*, which he coupled with a broad evolutionary naturalism. Besides being the principal author of the Manifesto, Sellars provided an intellectual foundation on which many humanists built. In order to understand neorealism and get a sense of the source of much humanist inspiration, Sellars's work in epistemology (his favorite subject) must be examined and then his theory of evolutionary novelty and emergence, noting finally his proposed resolution of the mind-body problem. Doing so will shed light on the implications these suggestions have for his religious perspective and hence for religious humanism.

Because Sellars found himself rooted in the materialist tradition, he stood firmly opposed to all forms of epistemological idealism. But he was not a naïve realist, either. In fact, his most profound contribution to American philosophy stems from his critique of naïve or natural realism and his substitution of critical or physical realism. And since epistemology defines all knowing, an understanding of critical realism is crucial to an appreciation of Sellars's religious postulates.

Natural realism may be described most simply as the common-sense view of perception. What we see when we look at an object is exactly what that object is; we see the surface of the object as it presents itself to us. We have no part in the perception except as the receptors of sensations that are accounted for by the object's existence. The object is totally independent of our awareness of it. Thus, the knower directly intuits knowledge of the things around him.

In one sense, natural realism is not a theory of knowledge but a practical description of what human beings find going on when they perceive. The scientific attitude takes many of the natural realist's points for granted. But sophisticated science must modify the description, and here is where Sellars entered the scramble. If we think about it a moment, we realize that physical things cannot *actually* enter and then disappear from our consciousness.

In the first place, we are aware that an object will appear different from different perspectives and under different conditions. How, then, can we intuit anything but appearance? We are also aware that what we see depends a great deal on what we expect to see, which is determined by cultural and social factors often beyond our control. So, how does natural realism explain dreams, fairy tales, and memories? The logician and psychologist tell us that perception is essentially judgmental.[36] With all these objections to natural realism, Sellars could hardly be expected to adopt it outright. Yet he thought it was the right starting point, certainly better than abstract, ethereal idealism. The assignment, then, was to remake realism.

What had to be maintained in the redoing process was the integrity of both the object and the knower. They both played a part in the operation, and any system that ignored that fact was bound to end up in nonsense. The object and the knower were co-real. The object existed in its own right, but in order for that object to be known, the knower had to be involved in the procedure.

At this point, Sellars introduced a distinction between sensation (sense-data) and perception. It is this distinction that *makes* his theory. The knower does, indeed, intuit sensory appearances that originate in the object itself. These sensations guide the knower, giving cues and suggestions about the nature of the object. But the process of knowing that object involves a second step: the act of perception or, in Sellars's terminology, "the denotative reference of the thing-object."

This is where the knower comes in. Taking cues and impressions from the received sense-data, the knower then adds the effects of his or her perspective, conditioning mindset, and so on to the process and, in this way, characterizes the thing-object in the final form in which we can say it is *known*.[37]

The total procedure is the process of knowing. Knowing is still a matter of process, as it is for the pragmatist, but a differently conceived process. In this way, Sellars escapes object-perceiver dualism. What is known is the external thing, but it is known by means of internal discrimination. The object is known directly but mediately. The public independence and reality of both thing and self are maintained because they coexist and the faults of naïve realism are avoided. It is an ingenious compromise.

What, then, is truth? In a broad sense, it is whatever gives knowledge of its object, which means that simple perception may not be enough. How do we know what has given accurate knowledge of its object? Here is where Sellars's reliance on science comes into play. There are, he says, different levels of knowing, each higher level capable of improving upon the lower. All knowing, since it is mediated by perception, is only approximate. But by controlling data and critically using perceptions, the scientist can come closer than the lay person to an accurate appraisal of external facts.[38]

Truth is what gives knowledge of its object, and we know a statement to be true if it corresponds to the state of affairs it is referring to. But the traditional correspondence theory of truth, in which appearance and reality coincide, is not for Sellars an adequate test of truth, as it was for the empiricists; it is simply an indication of the fact that we have knowledge.

If we recall what Sellars believes knowledge is, then correspondence simply expresses the fact that our knowledge is of *this* specific set of external objects rather than *that* set. Our knowledge corresponds, if it is true knowledge, with whatever set of sensations it refers to. The test of truth, on the other hand, is not correspondence (which is a criterion of truth, not a definitive test) but *praxis*. If we can effectively exercise control of our world in terms of our ideas, then we have knowledge—true knowledge—of it.

It may be clear now what Sellars's relationship to the pragmatists was. Unlike them, he could affirm a limited correspondence theory of truth because he believed that perception was, to some extent, under the causal control of the sense-data emanating from the particular corresponding object under consideration. But because he allowed sufficiently for the role of the human perceiver in the process, he could agree with the pragmatists' instrumental test of truth.[39] He believed with the pragmatists that human beings were agents, not mere spectators, and the brilliance of his work was that he wrote that agency into his epistemology in a way that accounted for our perceptual prejudices and our scientific modifications of them.

Sellars drew out several implications from his theory for religion. The role of human beings in the knowing process was firmly established. They were central to it; not only could it not go on without them, but their epistemological predispositions played an integral part in shaping how the world (and reality) was conceived and constructed.

More than that, Sellars's argument lifted science to a preeminent level as the most reliable way of acquiring knowledge. It effectively prevented religion from taking refuge in any form of idealism: Knowing was a human, natural act in which people were capable of grasping the nature of external things without the aid of a supplementary agent or realm. Sellars and pragmatism had reached several similar conclusions but via slightly different routes.

But probably the most important thing about Sellars's epistemology was that it permitted him to make a definitive and original response to the mind-body problem, the ancient philosophical debate as to whether our minds are constituted of something other than that of our material bodies. To understand that response, however, one must have some idea of Sellars's conception of nature.

## Evolutionary Naturalism

To put it succinctly, matter is all that matters—or at least, it is all that is. Sellars was a neomaterialist, for whom everything could be accounted for in terms of the characteristics and transformations of matter. He said, "Back of pomp and circumstance, back of love and beauty and tragedy and happiness lie—matter. In short, the physical is but another term for being, for existence."[40] Matter is and it endures. Sellars does distinguish between *primary and secondary endurants:* the first being equivalent to the stuff of being that can never be destroyed and the latter standing for those conglomerations of the former that can be separated out and rendered nonendurable and nonexistent. But matter as being (as the *primary endurant*) can never cease to exist. And it lies at the heart of Sellars's ontology. Of it, the universe is composed.[41]

And what is the nature of that universe? Sellars rejects the old mechanistic view of self-contained atoms impinging upon each other in accordance with rigid mechanical laws. Nature, for Sellars, is an all-inclusive, spatio-temporal system of which everything is a part. It is a dynamic, fluctuating, thick confluence in which new bodies arise and new properties emerge. Its whole acts different from its parts. And though there is no room in it for a divine agent, it is not an unfriendly place either. Sellars wrote, "It is the natural scene of birth and achievements. It is something within which to work in a human way."[42]

Part of our problem, Sellars contended, is that we have failed to think of our universe accurately and have been deceived into vitalizing and anthropomorphizing it in ludicrous ways. We have thought of time and space as entities and conditions in which we find ourselves, when, in fact, they are merely descriptions. Space is the measurability and localizability of things. Put simply by Sellars, "The physical world is not *in* space; it is spatial."[43] *Time* is simply a word for a sequence of events and the change that takes place within that sequence. It is not a condition segregated from matter; it is a characteristic of matter. There is, therefore, no need for a first event.[44]

Moreover, we have tended to think that natural order requires a cause or plan, when, in fact, it is simply intrinsic to nature. The universe is stuffed with complex units of multileveled organization. The organization or structure of matter is, in fact, just what differentiates one unit from another, one species or set from the next. Just as matter may move from a primary to a complex secondary endurant, so, in this process of patterning, may higher levels of organization emerge. And all this occurs without the intrusion of any master intelligence or purposeful external direction.

It is from this fact (that the universe encourages extended, sometimes cumulative, often diversified patternings at more and more complex levels) that the principle of novelty arises. (Sellars identified an analogical progression from inorganic nature to living things to mind and finally to civilization.)[45] We no longer need to account for change and development in nonnatural, nonmaterialistic terms. Nature possesses within itself all that is needed to explain the occurrences of new units. Sellars calls this activity *emergence* and understands the fact evolutionarily. Organic evolution suggests that change is simply variation and adjustment within nature and not part of a plan; the tendency of the universe to organize more complexly results at certain junctures in the emergence of novelty.[46]

In light of this construction, some further conclusions may be drawn for religion. If nature and matter, by the very fact of their composition and action, can supply all necessary explanations of order and change, there is no need for a conscious agent. Not only is the universe self-created, as the Manifesto claims, but it is also self-sustaining and self-directed. Meaning must be intrinsic or not at all. Sellars conceived of cosmic purpose as "a feature of a certain level of nature expressive of complex structures. This thickening of organization develops action-as-a-whole and the relative autonomy or spontaneity of life. Out of this organic matric, conscious purpose evolves."[47]

*Value* is added to that purpose by human decision. Beauty and meaning are rooted in human nature, not some supersensible reality introduced from above; they are expressions of human aspirations, as is the entire religious enterprise. Religion, for Sellars, is self-conscious human life functioning in the face of its problems in an interpretive and natural way.[48]

The implications for the religious life that Sellars drew from his philosophy are similar to those drawn by many of the other humanists. This is not surprising, since he was chosen to draft their famous document. But Sellars *starts* his thinking from a point different from that of the pragmatists, and it is instructive to see how he reached many of the same conclusions by an alternative passage. Then, too, Sellars places humanity at the pinnacle of the patterns of his emergent organization and, in this way, provided a philosophical/scientific foundation for the humanists' faith in the human creature. The human mind, after all, is the most complex development in the evolutionary spiral—one that had long been thought to present a special problem for the materialists. If Sellars could supply a satisfactory resolution of the mind-body dilemma, his system would be made even stronger.

## Mind-Body Dualism

Sellars included in the third point of the Manifesto a rejection of mind-body dualism, the importance of which (in religious terms) was to eliminate the concept of *soul* or *spirit* from the deliberations. If the mind is an entity separate and apart from the human body, then it may survive the body's decay, in which case immortality is an ever-present possibility. If the mind and body are interdependent, however, such survival is impossible. This is the most cogent relevance of the mind-body problem for the orthodox religionist (although for the humanist, the significance of monism was also that it maintained the organic view of life and matter).

The crux of the difficulty for the materialist is to account for consciousness. On one level, the mind is a physical category involving physical operations. This is the level/domain of the brain. But what about consciousness? We are all aware of it, and yet it hardly seems a solely physical experience. Sellars wanted to argue that consciousness is not a "stuff" in a physical sense but rather an awareness, an event, something that happens *in* (but not *to*) a human being. Basically, it is a physical phenomenon like everything else. But it is a *condition* created by a physical phenomenon (the brain and its corresponding nervous system) that human beings *experience* in a nonmaterialistic way. Is there a contradiction here?

Sellars thought not. This is a case of *double knowledge*. We can deny neither brain nor mind, neither the strictly physical operations of the nervous system nor the introspective operations of consciousness. The latter is not *apart* from the former; it is a distinct manifestation of the former. And both orientations are valid. Indeed, they *have* to be, since they are both part of our experience. As Sellars explained, "What I ask is that these two approaches be seen to *supplement* each other. . . . To assert that a cortical process is conscious is to assert that it *contains* the sort of experience we enjoy and contemplate introspectively . . . a work of synthesis needs to be done."[49]

Whether this is a successful resolution of mind-body dualism is largely another issue. But it was on this point that evolutionary naturalism came under fiercest attack. George Dodson, for instance, questioned how such a posture could be maintained in light of "the indisputable fact of . . . interaction" of mind and body.[50] But Sellars simply charged him with begging the question. Humanism has revised the notion of mind from "immaterial substance, or stream of ideas, to functional activities which are conscious," Sellars replied. The fact of interaction is superfluous.[51]

Robert Hutcheon, a professor at Meadville Theological School, devoted an entire book to the critique of humanism, a large part of which took on Sellars. Hutcheon claimed that the philosopher refused to allow any reciprocal interdependence between mind (consciousness) and brain (neural activity), to which Sellars responded, "[Consciousness] does not act from outside [the mind-brain system] because it is not outside nor is it a special form of energy. It is intrinsic to an awareness of pattern which is at one and the same time neuromental and conscious."[52] Hence, *reciprocal interdependence* is hardly the phrase: Consciousness and brain can hardly *become* interdependent if they are never separate in the first place.

Hutcheon's most telling criticism came in another area when he asked Sellars why emergents emerge.[53] To this, the humanist could only reply that such was the nature of being. He wrote in return, "I have refused to appeal to any principle but that of creative synthesis, the tendency to organization under favorable circumstances. The higher levels of evolution are local. Evolution does not apply to the universal collectively but only distributively and in parts. I am content to follow the facts in a pluralistic and empirical way."[54]

That is the way it is, said Sellars. Take it or leave it. Most of the humanists chose to take it.


This discussion has come a long way—from the Enlightenment, Huxley, Hegel, and the free religionists. The elemental sentiments that "man is the measure of all things," that knowledge is a developmental process, and that reality is a set of interrelated meanings found in nature have been refined, but their essential natures remain relatively untouched.

Within the Unitarian tradition, humanism inherited the respect for scientific authority that the Free Religious Association and the Western Unitarian Conference had nurtured in the late nineteenth century. But humanism's relationship with science was somehow more personal than the free religionists' because humanism recognized the part humanity played in the scientific enterprise. Reason—which had long been Unitarianism's "saint"—was replaced by human intelligence, and it was a cogent substitution. Humans no longer reasoned *about* nature and reality; by means of intervening intelligence, they now *participated* in their creation.

This idea is explicit in both Dewey's and Sellars's theories of knowledge. Humanism was in no sense a passive thought system, staring into space in search of inherent meaning. Having followed in Dewey's tracks, it conceived of intelligence as active problem solving and of humanity as the executive perpetrator of change (in collaboration, to be sure, with evolution). Regardless of whether it was a valid perspective, it had the advantage of assigning to human beings a dignity and elegance they had rarely been allowed in religious circles before.

# Endnotes

## Introduction

1. See, for example, Louis Menand's recent book on Oliver Wendell Holmes, William James, Charles Pierce, and John Dewey, *The Metaphysical Club* (New York: Farrar, Straus and Giroux, 2001).

2. I call religious humanism a *faith* throughout the book, even though some of its pioneers would not be happy with that appellation, convinced as they were that science grounded their every belief. But I would contend that science, too, is based on some *a priori* truths that must be taken on faith (for example, the assumption that the world is not a mere chimera invented by a churlish devil who has persuaded us that our sensory perceptions actually correspond to an independently existing reality).

3. "New Survey of UUs Shows Theological Differences, Common Values," *World* (May–June 1998): 36–37.

4. See William F. Schulz, "The Humanist Basis for Human Rights," *Humanist* (September–October 2000): 25–29; and William F. Schulz, *In Our Own Best Interest: How Defending Human Rights Benefits Us All* (Boston: Beacon Press, 2001), 17–37.

5. Sharon Begley, "Searching for the God Within," *Newsweek*, 29 January 2001, p. 59. This new field of research is called *neurotheology*.

6. Alfred North Whitehead, *Functions of Reason* (Princeton, NJ: Princeton University Press, 1929).

7. The humanists would claim, of course, that their reliance on science as the arbiter of truth neutralizes the stain of culture—the scientific method, in their view, transcending all cultural influences and, hence, rendering its findings valid in all contexts. Regardless of the merits of this claim, it may account for why many humanist Unitarian Universalists resist making room for other religious views within their congregations. Namely, the humanists' version of religious truth is supposedly validated by science, while those of other religions lack such a reputable source of authority.

8. Mark D. Morrison-Reed, *Black Pioneers in a White Denomination* (Boston: Beacon Press, 1984), 117.

9. Although only six signers were alive when I determined to take early religious humanism as my dissertation topic, I had interviewed a seventh, Oliver Reiser, in Pittsburgh in 1972, shortly before he died.

10. Wilson subsequently published his own version of the birth of the Manifesto, entitled *The Genesis of a Humanist Manifesto* (Amherst, NY: Humanist Press, 1995).

11. Sarah Oelberg, "The Faith of a Unitarian Universalist Humanist" (Boston: Unitarian Universalist Association, 2000).

## The Roots of Religious Humanism

1. Friedrich Nietzsche, "The Gay Science," in *The Portable Nietzsche*, ed. Walter Kaufmann (New York: Viking Press, 1984), 95–96.

2. Thomas Henry Huxley, "Agnosticism," in *Science and the Christian Tradition* (New York: D. Appleton, 1896), 245–46.

3. Ludwig Feuerbach, quoted in Karl Lowith, *From Hegel to Nietzsche* (Garden City, NY: Doubleday, 1967), 333.

4. Harry Emerson Fosdick, *The Meaning of Faith* (New York: Associated Press, 1919), 70.

5. Walter Lippmann, *A Preface to Morals* (Boston: Beacon Press, 1929), 21.

6. Kenneth Cauthen, *The Impact of American Religious Liberalism* (New York: Harper & Row, 1962), 74.

7. Henry Steele Commager, *The American Mind* (New Haven, CT: Yale University Press, 1950), 168–77.

8. Commager, *The American Mind*, 162–63.

9. Sidney Warren, *American Freethought: 1860–1914* (New York: Columbia University Press, 1943), 36–37.

10. Clarence Darrow, "If a Man Die," *Literary Digest* 100 (30 March 30 1929), 26–27.

11. George Santayana, "The Intellectual Temper of the Times," *Winds of Doctrine* (New York: Charles Scribner's Sons, 1912), 1.

12. James Truslow Adams, *Our Business Civilization* (New York: Albert & Charles Boni, 1929), 9–31.

13. Sidney Ahlstrom, *A Religious History of the American People* (New Haven, CT: Yale University Press, 1972), 900.

14. Frederick Lewis Allen, *Only Yesterday* (New York: Harper & Row, 1931), 177–78.

15. P. W. Slosson, *The Great Crusade and After, 1914-28* (New York: Macmillan, 1930), 428.

16. Slosson, *The Great Crusade and After*, 433.

17. Allen, *Only Yesterday*, 177–78.

18. Stewart Cole, *The History of Fundamentalism* (New York: R. R. Smith, 1931).

19. Christopher Lasch, *The Agony of the American Left* (New York: Random House, 1966), 33–60.

20. Joseph Wood Krutch, *The Modern Temper* (New York: Harcourt, Brace, 1929), 9.

21. Allen, *Only Yesterday*, 292.

22. E. A. Burtt, *Types of Religious Philosophy* (New York: Harper, 1939), 252–64.

23. Herbert W. Schneider, *Religion in 20th Century America* (New York: Atheneum, 1964), 152–53.

## The Emergence of Religious Humanism

1. Quoted in David B. Parke, ed., *The Epic of Unitarianism* (Boston: Beacon Press, 1957), 124.

2. Stow Persons, *Free Religion* (Boston: Beacon Press, 1947), 62

3. Quoted in Stow Persons, "Religion and Modernity," in *Evolutionary Thought in America* (New Haven, CT: Yale University Press, 1950), 380.

4. Charles Lyttle, *Freedom Moves West* (Boston: Beacon Press, 1952), 135.

5. Quoted in Lyttle, *Freedom Moves West*, 158.

6. Quoted in Lyttle, *Freedom Moves West*, 182.

7. Raymond B. Bragg, "Principles and Purposes of the Free Religious Association" (bachelor of divinity thesis, Meadville Theological School, 1930), 55.

8. Lyttle, *Freedom Moves West*, 256–58.

9. One of the problems with taking these dates (1917–1937) as definitive is that they represent events within Unitarian history and may fail to reflect the supra-Unitarian nature of the religious humanist movement. Since the history of religious humanism is focused in Unitarianism, we need simply keep its non-Unitarian aspects and contributors in mind while reviewing its Unitarian heritage.

10. See Appendix B.

11. See Frank C. Doan, "The Present God," in *Religion and Life* (chapel addresses by members of the faculty of Meadville Theological School) (Boston: Sherman, French, 1909), 57–65.

12. As minister of the First Unitarian Church of Rochester from 1922–1925, Doan put the whole matter succinctly: "In a word, religion for us has always begun at the human end." Quoted in Frank G. Doan, "The Human Side of Religion" (reprint of Sermon to First Unitarian Church of Rochester, New York, n.d.), 6.

13. J. A. C. Fagginner Auer, *Humanism States its Case* (Boston: Beacon Press, 1933).

14. Carleton Winston, *This Circle of Earth: The Story of John H. Dietrich* (New York: G. Putnam, 1942), 66–82.

15. Curtis Reese, "My Life among the Unitarians" (manuscript, 1961), 6.

16. Reese, "My Life among the Unitarians," 13.

17. Winston, *This Circle of Earth*, 121–22.

18. Interview with Lester Mondale (Copperhead Cliffs, MO, summer 1974).

19. John H. Dietrich, *Humanist Pulpit* (Minneapolis: First Unitarian Society, 1927–1937), vol. 1–8.

20. Harry Elmer Barnes, *The Twilight of Christianity* (New York: Vanguard Press, 1929), 455.

21. John H. Dietrich, "The Meaning of Modernism," *Humanist Pulpit* ser. 8, no. 7 (15 February 1925): 16.

22. John H. Dietrich, "Is the Universe Friendly or Unfriendly?" *Humanist Pulpit* ser. 14, no. 2 (21 September 1930): 36.

23. John H. Dietrich, "Of What Can We Be Certain?" *Humanist Pulpit* ser. 3, no. 8 (5 January 1919): 11.

24. John H. Dietrich, "Religion without God," *Humanist Pulpit* ser. 14, no. 1 (8 December 1929): 15.

25. John H. Dietrich, "The God of Evolution," *Humanist Pulpit* ser. 7, no. 5 (13 April 1924): 3–15.

26. John H. Dietrich, "Is Atheism a Menace?" *Humanist Pulpit* ser. 11, no. 2 (18 September 1928): 17–32.

27. John H. Dietrich, "My Religion," *Humanist Pulpit* ser. 12, no. 5 (9 December 1928): 75–76.

28. John H. Dietrich, "Meeting Trouble without God," *Humanist Pulpit* ser. 12, no. 3 (28 October 1928): 39.

29. Mason Olds, "Three Pioneers of Religious Humanism" (doctoral dissertation, Brown University, 1973), 95. This dissertation eventually became a book: *Religious Humanism in America: Dietrich, Reese, and Potter* (Lanham, MD: University Press of America, 1977). Considerable controversy has arisen over whether Dietrich renounced humanism in the waning years of his life. He retired in 1936 but remained active until close to the time of his death in 1957. It appears that as early as 1942, however, he was struggling anew with the viability of the faith. "What a hell of a world!" he wrote in a letter that year to Edwin Wilson. "One stands aghast at the utter madness. Humanism is the answer but it takes a lot of faith these days" (24 February 1942).

   Yet in 1948, Paul Kinney, newly appointed managing editor of the *Humanist*, reported after visiting Dietrich that he had affirmed, once again, that the central focus of religion is man—that it matters not what a person believes about God but that what is important is to work for humanist objectives (handwritten notes following meeting with Dietrich in Berkeley, CA, 28 November 1948).

Kinney's report may, however, reflect a distortion in Dietrich's thinking; the appointment had been set up by Wilson, who confided to Dietrich that Kinney "needs inspiration as his work has been slow to get underway and he feels discouraged." Dietrich may kindly not have wanted to discourage Kinney any further.

By the 1950s, in any case, Dietrich's philosophy does seem to have taken something of a turn. In a letter to Wilson, he regrets his having juxtaposed a God-controlled with a human-controlled world in his ministry. "I am now sorry because I realize how much richer and more effective a message I might have proclaimed if I had emphasized man's relation to the source of all being and the importance of communion with it" (10 October 1953) And a few months later, in a letter to a former parishioner, Dietrich elaborated, "[M]y philosophy and religion have undergone considerable revision in the past few years, especially in regard to . . . my dependence upon 'the Power behind Phenomena,' or God, if you please. I still hate to use the latter term because of the general misuse of it. I seek to develop a consciousness of this as a very important part of life." The elderly minister went on to repudiate science's ability to furnish religious or ethical values; finally, he went so far as to disown the most basic tenet of his humanism: "I recently read something which I think is true," he wrote. "'[A]ll of history has taught us that the denial of these ultimates [eternal truth, absolute morality, God], the placement of man . . . at the core of the universe, results in a paralyzing mass selfishness" (letter to "Dear Busey," copy to Wilson, 4 December 1953).

How much greater a departure from his previous views could we expect to witness? The last letter available, dated May 15, 1956 and addressed to another friend, reiterates many of these same points and adds, "I realize now how my utter reliance upon science and reason and my contempt for any intuitive insights and intangible values, which are the very essence of religion and art, was a great mistake; and the way in which I cut mankind off from all cosmic relationship, denying or ignoring every influence outside of humanity itself, was very short-sighted and arrogant." In describing his newly awakened appreciation of the "Power behind Phenomena," Dietrich went on to say, "I believe that by meditation we can experience its presence, bring ourselves into harmony with it, and find our lives enriched and energized." Commenting finally upon humanism— with which, he claimed, he no longer personally identified—he remarked, "I think Humanism had value as a protest movement with an emphasis upon human betterment, but its day has passed, and should be replaced by a more mature attitude toward the universe and human existence" (letter to Joseph S. Laughran, 15 May 1956).

Dietrich's apparent conversion did not go unnoticed. Many of his former parishioners were shocked and scandalized; some hoped to attribute his new views to senility. But in a memorable address delivered several months after Dietrich's death, Rev. Carl A. Storm, one of Dietrich's successors in Minneapolis, dispelled the rumor of senility by quoting from Dr. Raymond Cope, minister of the Berkeley Unitarian Church and a close friend of Dietrich's in his declining years: "[I]ntellectually," wrote Cope, "he was vigorous up to within a matter of days before his death. . . . Those persons who think that he became mentally soft in his later years simply do not know the facts." Cope's appraisal of Dietrich's mental facility is confirmed by the fact that until shortly before his death, Dietrich was studying Italian! (Carl A. Storm, "John H. Dietrich—A Tribute" [Minneapolis: First Unitarian Society, 1957], 12).

Whatever the reason for Dietrich's revised thinking, his new conclusions were hardly as radically out of line with his earlier version of humanism as some have suggested. In the letter of May 15, 1956, for instance, Dietrich details his new kind of religion as that which "arises from the consciousness of being a product and part of an all-powerful and all-penetrating force—God, nature, creative force—call it what you will, which is the dynamic of the whole universe, and which amid all the ups and downs of evolution and human history seems to drive toward improvement in every form, although frustrated by human ignorance. . . . Religion should seek to make people conscious of the fact that in every moment, . . . their lives are nourished, animated and urged toward better things by the inescapable presence of this all-enveloping power." These words are clearly similar to those found in much of Dietrich's humanist preaching. This is the cosmic power of his earlier days. Even some of the phrases are familiar.

Finally, Dietrich never dogmatically denied the existence of God and, indeed, described his position as that of "inquiry." That commitment to inquiry apparently lasted into his final days. At the time of his death, he was working on a manuscript entitled "Thoughts of God," in which he wrote, "I discard all dogmatic assurance. I do not even assert that I have made a discovery. But I am exploring. . . . The further I go the more I am conscious of the inconceivable vastness that lies beyond the borders of our knowledge " (quoted in Storm, "John H. Dietrich—A Tribute," 13).

Dietrich may have moved far from his earlier perspective, but he never turned his back on it entirely. Throughout his retirement years, even as late as December 1955, he made token contributions to the American Humanist Association to retain his membership and in a spirit of "goodwill" (letter to Edwin. H. Wilson, 9 December 1955). And in a 1953 symposium reassessing the Humanist Manifesto, he wrote, "[T]he positive side of Humanism was and is fine—its insistence upon the enrichment of life in its every form; but its negative side, cutting itself off from all cosmic relationship, . . . is very short-sighted." The Manifesto itself, he went on, "is definitely a dated document. . . . It in no ways reflects the humility that becomes the real seeker after truth. But that is the kind of fellows we were in those days. In fact I was one of the chief offenders" (see Storm, "John H. Dietrich—A Tribute," 13).

As he entered his twilight years, regretful of his youthful excesses, Dietrich's contemplation quite understandably moved in some alternative directions. That the "father of religious humanism" kept on exploring is evidenced by the fact that a few months before his death he eagerly discoursed with a visitor upon a new-found interest: Jean-Paul Sartre's existentialism! (interview with Edwin H. Wilson [Cocoa Beach, FL, summer 1974]).

30. Reese, "My Life among the Unitarians," 29. Reese goes on to say, "Prior to this [1916], . . . there were many sermons that were essentially humanistic in purpose and spirit, but the term humanism had not then come into vogue." These claims deserve two comments. In the first place, it was not Reese, but Dietrich, who brought the term *humanism* "into vogue." Reese was speaking most prominently of democratic religion and, in fact, changed the name of his first book from *Democratizing Religion* to *Humanism* under Dietrich's influence (Olds, "Three Pioneers of Religious Humanism," 48). Second, since Dietrich claims first to have preached a sermon on humanism in Spokane in early 1916, it is unclear which sermon was delivered earliest, since we have the exact date of neither. Furthermore, in his book *Freedom Moves West*, Lyttle writes, "As early as 1916, [I]

delivered a lecture at Cooper Institute in New York City on 'Humanism, America's Real Religion'" (see Lyttle, 243). In sum, there are at least three contenders for the honor of having been the first Unitarian minister to make a blatantly humanistic pronouncement.

31. Curtis W. Reese, *A Democratic View of Religion* (Yellow Springs, OH: American Humanist Association, n.d.). Even though Reese's statement was considered revolutionary at the time, it was not valued highly by all humanists. The iconoclastic Potter wrote of it in 1931, "Reese's 1918 sermon does not seem very challenging, but rather a run of the mill sermon on Unitarianism as a democratic religion" (letter to Edwin H. Wilson, 13 March 1931).

32. Olds, "Three Pioneers of Religious Humanism," 219.

33. Curtis Reese, *Humanism* (Chicago: Open Court, 1926), 6.

34. Curtis Reese, "The Faith of Humanism," *Open Court* 41 (May 1927): 277.

35. Curtis Reese, *Humanist Religion* (New York: Macmillan, 1931), 52.

36. See, for instance, Reese, *Humanism*, 10–12, 76–85.

37. Lyttle, *Freedom Moves West*, 244.

38. Curtis W. Reese, "Theism and Other Theories of God," *Christian Register* 105 (14 October 1926): 929.

39. Originally called "The Religion of Man," the title was changed by the *Register's* editor in order to make it less controversial.

40. John H. Dietrich, "The Religion of Experience," *Christian Register* 98 (13 March 1919): 241.

41. E. Burdette Backus, "Each for Himself Must Say," *Christian Register* 98 (8 May 1919): 437.

42. Emphasis in the original. Curtis W. Reese, "Do You Believe What He Believes?" *Christian Register* 99 (9 September 1920): 884.

43. Ironically, William G. Eliot was first cousin to Dr. Frederick May Eliot, whose election in 1937 to the AUA presidency can be considered the termination date of the humanist-theist controversy.

44. See pp. 15–18 in this book.

45. Reese, "My Life among the Unitarians," 50a.

46. Albert Dieffenbach, "A Theological Flurry," *Christian Register* 99 (22 July 1920): 711.

47. This remark is fairly typical of the humanist laypersons' democraticizing conceptions of the ministry and may be a clue as to why the Manifesto is so devoid of a distinctive doctrine of church and ministry.

48. Sidney S. Robins, "What Is a Humanist? This Will Tell You," *Christian Register* 99 (29 July 1920): 740.

49. Albert C. Dieffenbach, "Professor Sellars Again," *Christian Register* 99 (12 August 1920): 783.

50. Curtis W. Reese, "Western Conference Annual Meeting," *Christian Register* 100 (9 June 1921): 546.

51. Olds, "Three Pioneers of Religious Humanism," 59. Dodson, too, had a place on the WUC program, having addressed the May 17 ministers' luncheon on the topic "The Value of Theism." The ensuing discussion confirmed Reese's observation that "the ministers possess variety of beliefs as well as variety of gifts" (Reese, "Western Conference Annual Meeting").

52. George R. Dodson, "Clear Thinking or Death," *Christian Register* 100 (11 August 1921): 751.

53. Dodson, "Clear Thinking or Death," 751.

54. Dodson, "Clear Thinking or Death," 247

55. William L. Sullivan, "God, No-God, Half-God," *Christian Register* 100 (11 August 1921): 775–76.

56. Olds, "Three Pioneers of Religious Humanism," 62.

57. Richard W. Boynton, "Let Us Read History," *Christian Register* 100 (1 September 1921): 825–26.

58. George R. Dodson, "The Right of the Majority," *Christian Register* 100 (22 September 1921): 896.

59. Curtis W. Reese, "The Dead Hand," *Christian Register* 100 (1 September 1921): 826–27.

60. Frank C. Doan, "Dr. Dodson's Argument Seems Strange," *Christian Register* 100 (22 September 1921): 897–98.

61. Dodson, "The Right of the Majority," 896.

62. Dilworth Lupton, "Spiritual Reality and What Comes of It," *Christian Register* 100 (3 November 1921): 1040.

63. John H. Dietrich, "The Faith That Is in Us," *Christian Register* 100 (27 October 1921): 1014–15.

64. Dietrich, "The Faith That Is in Us," 1015.

65. Dietrich had made this same point in a sermon two and a half years before, when he had said of humanity's relation to the evolutionary Law of Progress, "[W]e may be certain . . . that through us alone can this Law of Progress continue to operate. . . . [A]ll progress, all success, life itself, depends upon bringing our work and habits into harmony with the laws of this universe" (Dietrich, "Of What Can We Be Certain?" 12).

66. William L. Sullivan, "The Faith That Makes a Church," *Christian Register* 100 (3 November 1921): 1039–40.

67. Sullivan, "The Faith That Makes a Church," 1040.

68. George R. Dodson, "The Man Who Spoke for Theism," *Christian Register* 100 (20 October 1921): 989–90.

69. Dietrich, "The Advance of Humanism," 39.

70. A. Wakefield Slaten, "Religion in the Making" (New York: Layman's League of West Side Unitarian Church, 1925), 7–8.

71. A. Wakefield Slaten, "A Spiritual Interpretation of Evolution" (New York: Layman's League of West Side Unitarian Church, 1925), 191.

72. A. Wakefield Slaten, "Social Progress" (New York: Layman's League of West Side Unitarian Church, 1926), 13–14.

73. A. Wakefield Slaten, "Religion without Revelation" (New York: Layman's League of West Side Unitarian Church, 1928), 14.

74. Slaten, "Religion in the Making," 15.

75. A. Wakefield Slaten, "A Philosophy of Life" (New York: Layman's League of West Side Unitarian Church, 1926), 8.

76. Charles Francis Potter, *The Preacher and I* (New York: Crown, 1951), 360.

77. Potter, *The Preacher and I*, 360–61.

78. The propositions of the four debates (and the winners) were as follows: (1) The Bible Is the Infallible Word of God (Potter); (2) The Earth and Man Came by Evolution (Stratton); (3) The Miraculous Virgin Birth of Jesus Christ Is a Fact and an Essential Christian Doctrine (Potter); and (4) Jesus Christ Is the Only Divine Son of God (Stratton). The fifth debate, on the Second Coming of Jesus, was never held.

79. John Roach Stratton and Charles Francis Potter, *Fundamentalist-Modernist Debates*, 4 vols. (New York: George H. Doran, 1924).

80. Olds, "Three Pioneers of Religious Humanism," 265. After all, in these debates, Potter was representing what was described then as the "modernist" Christian position.

81. Charles F. Potter, "Humanism—Theism," *Christian Register* 105 (26 April 1926): 396, 408.

82. Today, the Universalist Church of New York (Fourth Universalist Society).

83. Letter to Wilson, 13 March 1931.

84. Alfred R. Hussey, "Are Unitarians Christians?" *Christian Register* 105 (4 February 1926): 105–06.

85. Maxwell Savage, "A Letter Pertaining to Humanists," *Christian Register* 105 (15 February 1926): 131. In the Meadville Theological School library's copy of the issue of the *Register* in which Savage's article appears, the words "Phooey!" and "Boredom is Hell!" are penciled on the article page—apparently, unsolicited editorial comments from the humanist sympathizers of that day.

86. John H. Dietrich, "Humanism: By a Leading Exponent," *Christian Register* 105 (18 February 1926): 158. The most comprehensive statement on humanism in the *Register*'s pages since the 1921 conflict, this article was preceded by an editorial comment about the number of people who had requested such a piece.

87. "[A]nd should of course be properly disciplined," the sentence ended. Dietrich is probably referring to his address on "The Faith That Is in Us" and retracting any attempt to speak for the denomination. One suspects, however, that he was writing with tongue in cheek about *discipline*, for it is hard to believe that he favored any discipline.

88. John H. Dietrich, "Christian or Humanist?" *Christian Register* 105 (4 March 1926): 205.

89. Curtis W. Reese, "Appeal for Discrimination," *Christian Register* 105 (18 March 1926): 253, 266.

90. August Reccord, "From Dr. Reccord," *Christian Register* 105 (4 March 1926): 205.

91. William James, *Pragmaticism: A New Name for Some Old Ways of Thinking* (New York: Longmans, Green, 1949), 198.

92. "Dr. C. E. Park's View on Humanism," *Christian Register* 108 (23 May 1929): 444.

93. Namely, that the "relationship [between theism and humanism] is not antagonistic, but supplementary. Theism is humanism plus. It has all that humanism has, 'and then some.'" From Augustus Reccord, "Humanism Plus," *Christian Register* 106 (28 July 1927): 609.

94. W. Frank Swift, William Elsdon, Raymond B. Bragg, and Alfred W. Hobart, "'Theism Is Humanism Plus'?" *Christian Register* 106 (18 August 1927): 658–59.

## Bursting the Unitarian Bounds

1. The most prominent members of the second generation were probably Edwin H. Wilson (Meadville class of 1926) and Raymond B. Bragg (1927), but other active Meadville humanists included Harold Buschman (1928), later editor of the *New Humanist*; Alfred W. Hobart (1938); W. Francis Swift (1938), signer of the Humanist Manifesto; John G. MacKinnon (1930); and Melvin L. Welke (1930). Another prominent member of the new generation was Lester Mondale (Harvard class of 1929), originally a disciple of Dietrich and eventually the youngest signer of the Manifesto.

2.  Charles Lyttle, *Freedom Moves West* (Boston: Beacon Press, 1952), 253.

3.  A. Eustace Haydon, *Quest of the Ages* (New York: Harper & Bros., 1929), 1–27.

4.  A. Eustace Haydon, "The Reply," *New Humanist* 5 (July–August 1932): 13.

5.  Haydon, *Quest of the Ages*, 22.

6.  A. Eustace Haydon, "A Meditation on Modernists," *New Humanist* 5 (January–February 1932): 10.

7.  A. Eustace Haydon, "New World Religious Liberals Would Make," *Boston Evening Transcript*, 9 August 1924. In fairness to Haydon, he also called for stricter controls over the uses of science, saying, "The humanist recognizes that science in the hands of selfish men, allowed to create a civilization without the blessing or control of social idealism, has given us the modern age with its cruel maladjustments and its perversion of all human values" (A. Eustace Haydon, *Humanism* [San Francisco: Gilbert & Kroff, n.d.], 4). He also disparaged uncritical visions: "Idealism is sobered by knowledge. Utopias are outmoded. There is no longer a search for panaceas. . . . [T]here will always be problems and new forms of evil" (Haydon, *Quest of the Ages*, 148).

8.  The column was discontinued either because it was running short of material or because the magazine was taking on a more academic, supra-Unitarian, supra-ecclesiastical tenor, which made the devotion of space to the parochial and practical concerns of the clergy no longer appropriate.

9.  A. Wakefield Slaten, "The Humanist Pulpit," *New Humanist* 1 (November 1928): 5.

10. Edwin H. Wilson, "The Use and Abuse of Words in Inducing Religious Experience," *Meadville Journal* (ca. 1930). Wilson's thinking about language had been influenced by the work of Count Korzybski, a linguist who emphasized the importance of verbal candor and urged that we "say what we mean!" (Interview with Edwin H. Wilson [Cocoa Beach, FL, summer 1974]).

11. Lester Mondale, "The Second Generation Humanists," *New Humanist* 5 (July–August 1932): 1–8.

12. Interview with Lester Mondale (Copperhead Cliffs, MO, summer 1974).

13. James H. Hart, "The Lost Individual," *New Humanist* 5 (March–April 1932): 1–11.

14. James H. Hart, "A Religious Mood," *New Humanist* 6 (January–February 1933): 1–9.

15. *Unity* magazine was the publication of the Western Unitarian Conference and edited by John Haynes Holmes and Curtis W. Reese. It was also a source of humanist reflection, but not in the systematic way of the *New Humanist*.

16. H. G. Creel, "Thank You—And a Clarification," *New Humanist* 1 (May 1928): 2.

17. H. G. Creel, "The Program of the Humanist Fellowship," *New Humanist* 1 (May 1928): 1.

18. Charles Francis Potter to Harold Buschman and Edwin Wilson, 5 March 1931.

19. Harold Buschman, "Comment on the Humanist Manifesto," *New Humanist* 6 (May–June 1933): 29.

20. Harold Buschman to Charles Francis Potter, 19 March 1931. Wilson, a devoted institutionalist, came to differ with Buschman over whether humanism needed a visible organizational structure; Buschman feared that development would provoke a critical backlash.

21. These early editions of the *Humanist* carried the additional title of "New Series" in order to establish that they had directly descended from the early *New Humanist*.

22. Other activities of the original Humanist Fellowship included sponsorship of a lecture series in 1929 on the campus of the University of Chicago, which brought Professor T. V. Smith to speak on "Science and Government," Roy Wood Sellars on "Science and the Economic Order," and Haydon on "Science and Religion." Even though the event was planned to be an annual one, another series was apparently never held ("Lecture Series Successful," *New Humanist* 2 [May 1929]: 3).

One other agency for the promotion of humanism was the Humanist Extension Bureau, formed in fall 1932 by John Dietrich and a member of his congregation, Howard G. Kraus. Listing fifteen eventual signers of the Manifesto on its advisory committee, the Bureau intended to sponsor "a lecture tour embracing the entire country in conjunction with a general publicity and radio campaign" ("A Humanist Extension Bureau," *New Humanist* 5 [September–October 1932]: 29–30 and back cover). Whether it did is not known.

23. Mason Olds, "Three Pioneers of Religious Humanism" (doctoral dissertation, Brown University, 1973), 275.

24. Wallace Rusterholtz, *American Heretics and Saints* (Boston: Manthorne and Burack, 1938), 303.

25. Charles Francis Potter, *The Preacher and I* (New York: Crown, 1951), 361.

26. Potter, *The Preacher and I*, 356–68.

27. Wilson, interview.

28. Information sheet for Eldred C. Vanderlaan (Department of the Ministry, Unitarian Universalist Association, Boston, MA).

29. Wilson, interview.

30. Albert Dieffenbach, "Religion without God," *Christian Register* 106 (26 April 1928): 341–42.

31. "On Redefining God," *Christian Register* 105 (10 May 1928): 388.

## Making the Manifesto

1. Information sheet for Leon M. Birkhead (Department of the Ministry, Unitarian Universalist Association, Boston, MA).

2. "Dr. L. M. Birkhead Dies," [Kansas City] *Times*, 2 December 1954, 22.

3. Interview with Lester Mondale (Copperhead Cliffs, MO, summer 1974).

4. "On Trail of Sinclair Lewis Here," [Kansas City] *Times*, 18 June 1955.

5. Edwin H. Wilson, "Humanist Movement in the United States" (manuscript), 26. This point was also confirmed in a conversation with Raymond Bragg (St. Louis, MO, summer 1974).

6. Frederick Lewis Allen, *Only Yesterday* (New York: Harper & Row, 1931), 292–93.

7. Ernest Caldecott, "Dare Liberals Lead?" *Christian Register* 4 (5 January 1933): 8–9.

8. Curtis Reese, "Principles of Constructive Planning," *Christian Register* 4 (19 January 1933): 35–36.

9. That the Manifesto's fourteenth point was a depression-inspired item of faith is evidenced by the wholesale retreat from socialism that occurred among humanists in the early 1950s. (The Red-baiting atmosphere of those years was also responsible for humanist disclaimers.)

10. Charles Lyttle, *Freedom Moves West* (Boston: Beacon Press, 1952), 255.

11. Allen, *Only Yesterday*, 202–03.

12. Interview with Raymond Bragg (Kansas City, MO, summer 1974).
13. Bragg, interview.
14. A negative catalytic factor in the issuance of the Manifesto at this particular time was a desire on the part of the Chicago group to head off a more journalistic or promotional approach, such as Charles Francis Potter might spearhead. The more moderate, academically inclined humanists looked with disfavor upon some of Potter's campaigns and sought the respectability of a solidly grounded intellectual document (Interview with Edwin H. Wilson [Cocoa Beach, FL, summer 1974]; and Bragg, interview).
15. Raymond B. Bragg, "An Historical Note," *Humanist* 13 (March–April 1933): 62.
16. Wilson, "Humanist Movement," 39.
17. Wilson, "Humanist Movement," 41.
18. Wilson, "Humanist Movement," 34–35.
19. Bragg, interview.
20. Wilson, "Humanist Movement," 41–42.
21. Burtt no doubt felt compelled to beg the committee to withhold publication, because his letter was dated the day upon which he had requested all signatures be received. Burtt's request for a delay, nevertheless, was successful.
22. Edwin A. Burtt to Raymond B. Bragg, April 10, 1933.
23. Edwin A. Burtt to Raymond B. Bragg, April 12, 1933.
24. Edwin A. Burtt to Raymond B. Bragg, April 12, 1933.
25. Edwin A. Burtt to Raymond B. Bragg, April 12, 1933.
26. Edwin H. Wilson to John Herman Randall, Jr., April 17, 1933.
27. Edwin A. Burtt to Raymond B. Bragg, April 12, 1933.
28. John Herman Randall, Jr., to Edwin H. Wilson, April 18, 1933.
29. Edwin A. Burtt to Raymond B. Bragg, April 12, 1933.
30. Edwin H. Wilson to John Herman Randall, Jr., April 17, 1933.
31. Wilson, "Humanist Movement," 76.
32. Robert Morse Lovett to Raymond Bragg, April 20, 1933.
33. Edwin A. Burtt, "My Path to Philosophy," *Philosophy East and West*, 22, no. 4 (October 1972): 430–31.
34. The first public draft accompanied Bragg's letter of approximately April 1. Only a select group received a second draft in mid-April, which contained many of Burtt's proposals.
35. Roy Wood Sellars, "Religious Humanism," *New Humanist* 6 (May–June 1933): 12.
36. The last two sentences are as follows: "Man is at last becoming aware that he alone is responsible for the realization of the world of his dreams, that he has within himself the power for its achievement. He has only to set intelligence and will to the task."
37. John Herman Randall, Jr., to Edwin H. Wilson, April 18, 1933.
38. Wilson, "Humanist Movement" 186. See also p. 46 and p. 98 in this book.
39. Raymond Bragg to John Dewey, April 13, 1933.
40. Llewelyn Jones taught journalism briefly, too, but teaching was not his major vocation. V. T. Thayer, although initially a professor, spent most of his life in educational practice as an administrator and theorist.
41. "Comment on Humanist Manifesto," *New Humanist* 6 (May–June 1933): 29.
42. "Comment on Humanist Manifesto," 33.
43. "Comment on Humanist Manifesto," 29–30.

44. "Comment on Humanist Manifesto," 29–30.
45. Wilson, "Humanist Movement," 118.
46. Schiller's pragmatic humanism did play a small role in developing religious humanism.
47. Harlow Shapley to Raymond R. Bragg, April 21, 1933.
48. Frank H. Hankins to Edwin H. Wilson, May 25, 1933.
49. Bragg, interview.
50. Quoted in *U.U. World,* 1 October 1974, 4.
51. Bragg told of attending a luncheon with Russell where the Englishman is purported to have said that he was willing to posit a God who had never revealed himself to a single human soul and who on judgment day would damn any individual who had believed in him on insufficient evidence (Bragg, interview).
52. These signatories held Unitarian fellowship: J. A. C. Fagginer Auer, E. Burdette Backus, Leon Birkhead, Raymond Bragg, Ernest Caldecott, Albert C. Dieffenbach, John Dietrich, Harold Marley, Lester Mondale, Curtis W. Reese, W. Frank Swift, Eldred C. Vanderlaan, Frank S. C. Wicks, David Rhys Williams, and Edwin H. Wilson.
53. Quoted in *New Humanist* 6 (January–February 1933): 45.
54. Wilson, "Humanist Movement," 155.
55. Rabbi Joseph Baron to Raymond R. Bragg, April 24, 1933. Baron also said in his reply to Bragg, "I believe that it is repressive and futile . . . to establish a uniformity of opinion in a dynamic religious movement, particularly at such an early stage in its development."
56. It is worth noting that in the late 1960s, Rabbi Sherwin Wine founded the first Humanist Jewish temple in Birmingham, Michigan, and several others exist today across the United States.
57. Wilson, "Humanist Movement," 92.
58. Bruce Swift to Raymond Bragg, April 6, 1933.
59. Hugh Tigner to Raymond Bragg, April 5, 1933.

## Return to the Fold

1. Charles Francis Potter to Raymond Bragg, May 1, 1933.
2. Charles Francis Potter to Raymond Bragg, April 7, 1933.
3. "Humanism on Paper," *Time* 21 (15 May 1933): 48.
4. "For a New Religion—Humanism," *Literary Digest* 115 (20 May 1933): 20.
5. Leslie Pennington, "The Humanist Manifesto," *Christian Register* 112 (25 May 1933): 334.
6. John van Schaik, "A Humanist Manifesto," *Christian Leader* 36 (13 May 1933): 580–81.
7. "A Humanist Manifesto," *Standard,* 221.
8. The phrase "a living Power, or Process, or Something" was a perfect example of what humanism considered the modernist tendency to obfuscate. Why the *Century* hesitated to call the referent of its thought *God* is hardly clear.
9. "The Humanist Manifesto," *Christian Century* 50 (7 June 1993): 743–45.
10. Ibid.
11. Raube Walters, "The Theists' Rejoinder," *Christian Register* 112 (8 June 8 1933): 366.
12. Ernst Troeltsch, *The Social Teaching of the Christian Churches* (New York: Macmillan, 1931), 336.

13. Some of the signers' fathers were ministers, but they were either rural or missionary types and therefore similarly deprived of status.

14. While there are exceptions to this characterization (Floyd and Walker, for instance), the trait appears so regularly as to be more than accidental.

15. Melvin Seeman, "On the Meaning of Alienation," *American Sociological Review* 24 (November 1959): 788–89.

16. Robert Merton, "Social Structure and Anomie," in *Social Theory and Social Structure* (Glencoe, IL: Free Press, 1957), 144–45.

17. Charles Y. Glock, "The Role of Deprivation in the Origin and Evolution of Religious Groups," in *Religion and Social Conflict*, ed. Robert Lee and Martin Marty (New York: Oxford, 1964), 28.

18. J. Milton Yinger, *The Scientific Study of Religion* (New York: Macmillan, 1970), 276. It has already been noted that the Manifesto is both a theological (metaphysical) and a political document and that the *New Humanist* had endorsed Norman Thomas.

19. Glock, "The Role of Deprivation," 31.

20. Richard Hofstadter, *Anti-Intellectualism in American Life* (New York: Random House, 1962), 47.

21. Glock, "The Role of Deprivation," 35.

22. Interview with J. Milton Yinger (Oberlin, OH, summer 1974).

23. Luther P. Gerlach and Virginia H. Hines, "Five Factors Crucial to the Growth and Spread of a Modern Religious Movement," *Journal for the Scientific Study of Religion* 7 (Spring 1968): 23–24.

24. Charles Francis Potter to Edwin H. Wilson, undated (ca. 1939–1940).

25. In 1963, the American Humanist Association formally repudiated the fourteenth point.

26. "The Humanist Manifesto: Twenty Years After," *Humanist* (August 1953): 63–71.

27. Ibid.

28. Andrew Banning, "Confidence in Values," *Christian Register* 112 (6 July 1933): 437–39; Roy Wood Sellars, "Does Humanism Support Confidence in Values?" *Christian Register* 112 (7 September 1933): 586; and Andrew Banning, "Humanism and Subjectivism," *Christian Register* 112 (7 September 1933): 587.

29. Louis Harap, "The Paradox of Ethical Naturalism," *Christian Register* 112 (21 September 1933): 611–12; and John Dewey, "Comment on Ethical Naturalism," *Christian Register* 112 (28 September 1993): 639.

30. Joseph Haroutunian, "Humanism and Christianity," *Christian Register* 112 (26 October 1933): 691–93; J. A. C. Fagginer Auer, "Comment on Humanism and Christianity," *Christian Register* 112 (2 November 1933): 709–10: and Joseph Haroutunian, "In Reply to Professor Auer," *Christian Register* 112 (9 November 1933): 726–27.

31. J. A. C. Fagginer Auer and Julian Hartt, *Humanism versus Theism* (Yellow Springs, OH: Antioch Press, 1951).

## Appendix A: The Signers of the Humanist Manifesto

1. *General Catalogue of Meadville Theological School, 1844–1944* (Chicago: Meadville Theological School, 1945).

2. See, for example, E. Burdette Backus, "Each for Himself Must Say," *Christian Register* 98 (8 May 1919): 437, which was published during his ministry in Erie, PA.

3. Ministerial record sheet (Department of the Ministry, Unitarian Universalist Association, Boston, MA).

4. "What Is Friends of Democracy?" (pamphlet, no date), 3.

5. Interview with Raymond Bragg (Kansas City, MO, summer 1974).

6. Edwin A. Burtt, "My Path to Philosophy," *Philosophy East and West* 22 (October 1972), 429.

7. Interview with Edwin Burtt (Ithaca, NY, summer 1974).

8. Ministerial record sheet.

9. See, for example, Ernest Caldecott, *Studies in Liberalism* (Los Angeles: First Unitarian Church, 1944).

10. Ernest Caldecott, "Some Implications of Humanism," reprinted from *Religious Education* (November 1930).

11. Interview with Edwin H. Wilson (Cocoa Beach, FL, summer 1974).

12. *Bulletin for Medical Research* 2 (November–December 1956), 5.

13. Edwin H. Wilson, "Bernard Fantus: A Life of Kindness Guided by Intelligence," funeral address delivered April 16, 1940, in the Third Unitarian Church of Chicago.

14. William Floyd, "Truth and Democracy" (undated/post-1940), 8.

15. William Floyd, "The New Religion," *Arbitrator* 7 (November 1925): 1–3. The *Arbitrator* always carried these words at the bottom of the front page: "If misstatement of fact occurs, a correction from one better informed will be welcome." Of "The New Religion," Floyd wrote that "true religion is independent of physical occurrences of the past; that science has come nearer to truth than has theology; that the more accurate our knowledge of material facts, the more beneficent may become our metaphysics; and that the loftiest . . . ideas may be retrieved from contemplating the world around us."

16. In a memorial address for Floyd, Holmes said, "[T]here was always in William Floyd a certain spirit of rebellion against the status quo. One of his ancestors, whose name he bore, was a signer of the Declaration of Independence and that man's rebellious blood flowed ever in his veins. He was a pacifist—or peace patriot, as he would prefer to call it—and thus an outcast in time of war. He was thrice a heretic. Put humanism, socialism, and pacifism together, and you have the holy trinity of heresy" (quoted in *New York Times*, 27 November 1943).

17. Humanist Pioneer Award Citation.

18. Llewelyn Jones, "Grundtvig as a Scandinavian Precursor of Humanism," *Humanist* 13 (1953): 34–36.

19. Interview with Harold Marley (Hot Springs, AR, summer 1974).

20. Harold Marley, "When Humanism Becomes a Religion," *Humanist* 4 (Spring 1944): 24–26.

21. Interview with Lester Mondale (Copperhead Cliffs, MO, summer 1974).

22. Oliver Reiser, "Project Prometheus and Krishna," *World Union*, April–May–June 1970 (reprint).

23. Oliver Reiser, *Man's New Image of Man* (Pittsburgh: Boxwood Press, 1961), 61.

24. Interview with Oliver Reiser (Pittsburgh, PA, spring 1972).

25. Interview with Clinton Lee Scott (Mattapoisett, MA, summer 1974).

26. Scott, interview.

27. Roy Wood Sellars, "Realism, Naturalism, and Humanism," in *Contemporary American Philosophy*, eds. G. P. Adams and W. P. Montague (New York: Mac-Millan, 1930), 2: 261–85.

28. Sellars, "Realism, Naturalism, and Humanism," 263.

29. W. Francis Swift, "Neohumanism as Religious Philosophy" (bachelor of divinity thesis, Meadville Theological School, June 1928), 65.

30. *General Catalogue.*

31. Interview with Vivian T. Thayer (Arlington, VA, summer 1974).

32. Ministerial record sheet.

33. Joseph Walker, *Humanism as a Way of Life* (New York: Macmillan, 1932), 70.

34. Frank S. C. Wicks, "Good Men in Hell," American Unitarian Association pamphlet no. 275, (Boston: AUA, January 1914). This tract was not a humanist brief but a statement that appealed to larger Unitarianism. It began, "Every good man wants to go to hell. Only a bad man would want to go to heaven."

35. David Rhys Williams, *Faith beyond Humanism* (New York: Philosophical Library, 1963), viii.

36. David Rhys Williams, "Humanism and Mysticism," *Christian Register* 112 (30 November 1933): 775–76.

37. Roy Wood Sellars, "Humanism or Theism," *Christian Register* 112 (30 November 1933): 777–78.

38. Wilson, interview.

## Appendix B: The Philosophy of Religious Humanism

1. William James, *Principles of Psychology*, 2 vols. (New York: Henry Holt, 1890).

2. Joseph L. Blau, "Introduction," in William James, *Pragmatism and Other Essays* (New York: Washington Square Press, 1963), xi–xii.

3. James, *Pragmatism*, 89.

4. James, *Pragmatism*, 35.

5. James, *Pragmatism*, 212.

6. Humanism owed James other debts, such as his insistence upon a pluralistic conception of the world (which they would avow); his objections to atomistic materialism (a philosophy that Sellars, too, would criticize and replace with his own version); his criticism of absolutistic conceptions of deity and theism; and his influence upon Dewey.

7. Reuben Abel, *The Pragmatic Humanism of F. C. S. Schiller* (New York: King's Crown Press, 1955), 7–8.

8. Reuben Abel, ed., *Humanistic Pragmatism: The Philosophy of F. C. S. Schiller* (New York: Free Press, 1966), 66.

9. F. C. S. Schiller, *Humanism: Philosophical Essays* (London: Macmillan, 1903), xix.

10. Abel, *Humanistic Pragmatism*, 72–73.

11. John Dewey, *Experience and Nature* (Chicago: Open Court, 1925), 28.

12. Henry Nelson Wieman and Bernard Meland, *American Philosophies of Religion* (New York: Harper & Bros., 1936), 281.

13. John Dewey, *Reconstruction in Philosophy* (New York: Henry Holt, 1920), 122.

14. John Dewey, *A Common Faith* (New Haven: Yale University Press, 1934).

15. Dewey, *A Common Faith*, 86.

16. A. Eustace Haydon, *The Quest of the Ages* (New York: Harper & Bros., 1930).

17. Care must be taken to avoid confusion between the materialism that humanism rejected (which is better called *atomism*) and the neomaterialism (or *physical realism*) that Sellars proposed and that was widely affirmed.

18. Curtis Reese, *Humanist Religion* (New York: Macmillan, 1931), 17.

19. Max C. Otto, "The World Man Lives In," in *Man and His World*, ed. Baker Brownell (New York: Nostrand, 1929), 30.

20. Haydon, *The Quest of the Ages*, 203.

21. Max C. Otto, *Things and Ideals* (New York: Henry Holt, 1924), 209–10, 212. The emphasis upon utility in this passage recalls the philosophical roots of the movement in James and Schiller.

22. Curtis Reese, *Humanism* (Chicago: Open Court, 1926), 16.

23. Reese, *Humanism*, 78.

24. Curtis Reese, ed., *Humanist Sermons* (Chicago: Open Court, 1927), xiii.

25. J. A. C. F. Auer, *Humanism States Its Case* (Boston: Beacon Press, 1933), 51.

26. Reese, *Humanist Sermons*, ix.

27. Reese, *Humanism*, 25.

28. Haydon, *The Quest of the Ages*, 228–29.

29. John Dewey, *Human Nature and Conduct* (New York: Henry Holt, 1922).

30. Haydon, *The Quest of the Ages*, 175.

31. Oliver Reiser, "Scientific Humanism and the Crisis in Civilization," in *The Promise of Scientific Humanism* (New York: Oskar Priest, 1940), 238–46.

32. Curtis W. Reese, *The Meaning of Humanism* (Boston: Beacon Press, 1945).

33. John Dewey, *The Quest for Certainty* (New York: G. P. Putnam's Sons, 1929), 278.

34. Haydon, *The Quest of the Ages*, 141.

35. Reiser, "Scientific Humanism," 243.

36. Roy Wood Sellars, *The Principles and Problems of Philosophy* (New York: Macmillan, 1926), 44.

37. Roy Wood Sellars, *Critical Realism* (Chicago: Rand McNally, 1916).

38. C. F. Delaney, *Mind and Nature* (Notre Dame, IN: University of Notre Dame Press, 1969), 168–69.

39. Delaney, *Mind and Nature*, 170–72.

40. Roy Wood Sellars, *The Philosophy of Physical Realism* (New York: Macmillan, 1932), 6.

41. Norman Melchert, *Realism, Materialism, and the Mind* (Springfield, IL: Charles C Thomas, 1968), 117–20.

42. Roy Wood Sellars, *Religion Coming of Age* (New York: Macmillan, 1928), 156.

43. Sellars, *Religion Coming of Age*, 168.

44. Roy Wood Sellars, *Evolutionary Naturalism* (New York: Russell & Russell, 1922), 83ff.

45. Sellars, *Principles and Problems*, 345.

46. Sellars, *Evolutionary Naturalism*.

47. Sellars, *Religion Coming of Age*, 226.

48. Roy Wood Sellars, *The Next Step in Religion* (New York: Macmillan, 1918).

49. Sellars, *Physical Realism*.

50. George Dodson, "What the Manifesto Lacks," *New Humanist* 6 (September–October 1933): 30.

51. Roy Wood Sellars, "In Defense of the Manifesto," *New Humanist* 6 (November–December 1933): 11.

52. Roy Wood Sellars, "Humanism Viewed and Reviewed," *New Humanist* 4 (July–August 1931): 15–16.

53. Robert Hutcheon, *Humanism in Religion Examined* (Chicago: Meadville Theological School, 1931).

54. Sellars, "Humanism Viewed," 16.

# Index